Astoria Ghosts

By Jefferson Davis
With contributions
by the Advanced
Ghost Hunters
Of Seattle
Tacoma

Published by Norsemen Ventures

Davis, Jefferson Dale
  Astoria Ghosts
    1. Ghosts and Paranormal
    2. Spirituality and Mythology
    3. Local History
    4. Includes Index

Library of Congress Control Number: 2006911322

ISBN: 1-893186-10-5
    978-1893186-10-1

Acknowledgements

Many people contributed to this book, my first stop was at the Astoria-Hammond Chamber of Commerce, thank you Skip, Regina, Barb, Steve, Kelsey, and Sharon. Thanks to the Compleat Photographer for letting me use some of your wonderful historic photographs of Astoria.

The people of the Clatsop County Historical Society spent a lot of time talking with me, educating me about Astoria's History. Thanks to the docents and administrators at the Uppertown Firefighter's Museum, the Heritage Museum, and the Flavel House. I want to especially thank Martha, Mac, Sam, Liisa, and Joan.

The people of Astoria opened their homes and historic buildings to me as I did my research. I spoke to many staff members at the Hotel Elliott, thanks Chester, Ken and Sue Wilson, Julie, Jody, Ana, and Brenda.

Thanks to Rosemary and Larry at the Liberty Theater. Thank you Nancy, for letting me tour your pest house at Knappton Cove. Robyn, thanks for sharing your experiences at Fort Stevens.

Thanks to Sue and Steve, the owners of the Officer's Inn, you helped us with your knowledge about the history of the area. I know that Laurie was a bit scared by some of the events at the Officer's Inn and the Rosebriar Inn, but she and Janice told me of their experiences.

Last but not least, thanks to the paranormal investigators from the Advanced Ghost Hunters of Seattle, Tacoma (AGHOST), including Ross Allison, Patricia Davisson, Merlyn Ahern, Madeline Clayton, Racheal Ogan, Natalie Giles, Joey Greenfield, Gayla Lord, Donna Cirincione, Jill Thompson, Jody Cassady, and Stephanie Davisson. Thank you Karan, my psychic consultant. Thanks Jeff Belanger for your knowledge of Catholic orders.

I know I am missing some folks, so please forgive me if I did. I owe so much to so many.

Foreword

A woman was driving down the Lewis and Clark Road, when she felt something in the car with her... Another woman told me that sensitive people walking around downtown Astoria late at night could almost see the ghosts of past townspeople on the streets and in the buildings...

The written history of Astoria begins with the Lewis and Clark Expedition, making Astoria the oldest European-American settlement in Oregon. Apart from written history, the people of Astoria remember the hopes and tragedies of their ancestors, in many stories of ghosts and spirits. I had the privilege to speak with many of Astoria's citizens, who shared just a few stories about their city to include in this book.

As time goes by I hope to return to Astoria to hear more stories of ghost ships, sea monsters, ghostly soldiers, and haunted houses. I hope you enjoy these stories as much as I enjoyed learning of them.

Jefferson Davis

Table of Contents

Chapter 1

Astoria History

Native American Spirits

Thousands of years before Lewis and Clark spent a wet winter near the Pacific coast, Native Americans lived nearby. They traveled along the Columbia River, gathering plants, and the bounty of the sea. This included harvesting shellfish, catching salmon, and steelhead as the fish made regular runs up the river. The native peoples also caught seals and otter, as well as the occasional whale. A vast trade network connected the coastal people with the folk in the interior of the Pacific Northwest. They lived in winter villages of large houses made of cedar planks, feasting on the food they gathered and stored, earlier in the year.

Life could be harsh; the coast was a rich area, which they protected from enemy raiders. They also risked their lives on a daily basis, gathering the resources of an unforgiving sea. Even when they were not in their boats, the coastal people endured the cold and damp Pacific winters. Despite these drawbacks, the Native American lifestyle allowed them to develop a rich spiritual heritage.

To the coastal people, there was no difference between real animals, humans, and supernatural beings. Native Americans recognized the difference between a past, mythical age, and the present, modern one. Even so, the beings described in these past times were just as real as those that exist today.

They believed in a large number of spirits, including a Great God, the Raven, and many Elip Tillicum, or demi-gods. Depending upon the legend and tribe, each of these beings gave humanity fire and many other inventions. These beings could be unpredictable though. Some could aid one person on day, and torment another the next.

Many cultures place less emphasis on natural laws or accidents than our own. If a hunter went out looking for game and missed a shot at a fat deer, a supernatural being or an evil sorcerer may have spoiled his aim. People did not die of old age or natural causes. They died as a punishment for a sin, or from supernatural influences. Indeed, to most Native Americans magic was a natural force. If trees died, some entity, natural or supernatural may have had something to do with it. If a rock fell down a cliff, killing a hiker, someone, or something must have thrown it. They also believed in the spirits of the dead.

Many people of the Pacific Northwest believed in two lands of the dead. After people died, they traveled to the first, which was a kind of purgatory. The dead could not pass on, until their flesh and bones disappeared. The spirit stayed in this purgatory during the day, but at night, they returned to the world of living men. They often appeared to friends and relatives in dreams, begging the living to join them in the dead land. These ghosts sometimes cursed family and friends, taking them to the spirit world.

After the body disintegrated, its spirit passed over a river, into a second country west of the purgatory realm. Once there, it could not return to the world of the living.

Because of the danger of ghosts, most people buried their dead far away from any villages. Many of the islands on the Columbia River became cemeteries. Some native peoples built death houses there for the bodies. Once on the island, the spirits could not cross the water to return to their former villages. Some people buried their dead under the ground, or under cairns of rock. Other Native Americans put their dead in canoes on platforms or sometimes hung in trees. Once the body deteriorated in the canoe, it might be buried. Sometimes the canoe fell into the river, and sailed down the river into the afterlife

In the 1800s, a settler in Astoria married a native woman, who later fell into a coma. They thought she was

dead and gave away or burned all of her possessions. When she woke up, she told of being in a land of sunshine, where she had spoken with friends that had died before. They had told her that she did not belong there yet, and sent her back to the world of the living.

European and American Settlement

The channel where the Columbia River empties into the Pacific Ocean is a treacherous place. Hundreds of ships have been lost on the sandbars and tidal currents there. In the 18th Century, many Western explorers sailed past the river without recognizing it. Those who saw it could not sail through the channel. Captain Robert Gray tried several times, until on 11 May 1792, he found a way through the current and sand bars that guarded the river mouth. He anchored near modern Astoria, trading with the Indians who lived nearby. He named the great river the Columbia, after his ship, the *Columbia Rediviva*.

Captain George Vancouver followed Gray, sending one of his ships, the *Chatham*, over the sand bar, on 19 October that same year. The *Chatham's* commander Lieutenant William Broughton, did not feel safe sailing his ship further up river. He provisioned two of his ships boats with food and rowed upriver. He made his way east, near modern Troutdale, Oregon before he turned back. Before he left, Broughton made formal claim to the Columbia River territory for England.

Thirteen years later, Lewis and Clark made their way to the Pacific Northwest, traveling overland. They spent several days exploring the north and south bank of the Columbia, before choosing a winter campsite south of modern Astoria. They called the place Fort Clatsop. During the winter of 1805, into the spring of 1806, the expedition stayed at Fort Clatsop before heading east, toward St. Louis. These expeditions paved the way for later European and American settlement near Astoria.

Replica of Fort Clastsop

The Astorians

The Pacific Fur Company, was the first organization to set up a permanent trading post at the mouth of the Columbia River. The employees called themselves the Astorians, in tribute to their employer, John Jacob Astor. In the race to establish a trade network, Astor sent two groups to the mouth of the Columbia River, one by sea, and the other by land. On 11 March 1811, the *Tonquin* reached the mouth of the Columbia River. The Astorians set up their major trading post and warehouse on the south side of the river. They called it Fort Astor, after building a blacksmith shop, warehouse, office, and barracks. They set up several canon around their settlement. This made Astoria the oldest Euro-American settlement in Oregon. The overland expedition arrived at Fort Astor in February 1812. The *Beaver*, a resupply and trading ship also arrived in May, with more goods and men.

They beat the British owned Northwest Company, who set out from their trading post near modern Spokane.

The two groups agreed to coexist, the Hudson's Bay Company was a greater threat to both. Who knows where the competition would have gone, but for other world events? That same year, the United States joined in the conflict that Americans know as the War of 1812.

In January 1813, word reached Fort Astor that the United States and England were at war. The fighting had not reached the Pacific Northwest, but the Astorians worried. Britain controlled the seas, and could stop American ships from reaching Astor, or seize the post. On 16 October, a delegation from the North West Company purchased the fort and all of the Pacific Fur Company's interests in the Pacific Northwest for $58,000. The North West Company renamed the post Fort George. After the sale, the *HMS Raccoon* arrived, ready to storm Fort Astor for King and Country. The *Raccoon's* crew were a bit upset that it was already in British hands.

In 1814, the Treaty of Ghent ended the War of 1812. Most history books say that Astoria became a United States property then, or in 1818, when the Anglo American Convention of 1818 allowed joint ownership of the Oregon

Replica of Fort Astor in downtown Astoria, Oregon

Territory. It is a historic irony that under either treaty had the *Raccoon* seized Fort Astor; the British would have been required to return it to the Pacific Fur Company and pay reparations.

Because the Astorians sold it first, no matter how coercive the deal was, the matter was closed. Astor did not pursue the fur trade any further. This effectively ended any United States involvement in the fur trade of the Oregon Country for several years.

From 1813 to 1821, the Hudson's Bay Company and the North West Company competed for furs in the Pacific Northwest. In 1821, the North West Company merged into the Hudson's Bay Company. In 1824, Doctor John McLoughlin became the Chief Factor, or regional manager for the Pacific Northwest. He moved the company's base of operations up the Columbia River, and built Fort Vancouver in 1825. The United States had taken an interest in the Oregon Territory again, and he hoped the dividing line would become the Columbia River. He wanted his major trading post on the north side of the River to justify this claim

When McLoughlin and his employees left Fort George, they opened the way for United States merchants and fishermen to settle at the site of Fort George. The Native American villagers who lived nearby were decimated by a series of plagues. The handful of survivors abandoned many of their villages, centering themselves in the core of their traditional territories. A few Americans and other foreigners settled in the area, but they were few in number until the 1840s.

In 1846, the United States and Great Britain settled the international boundary line along the 49th Parallel, far north of the Columbia River. In 1847, Astoria had the first United States Post Office west of the Rocky Mountains. By 1850, over two hundred and fifty people lived in Astoria. In the 1850s, the United States began allowing its citizens to file Donation Land Claims of up to six hundred and forty acres of land. Many of the new Astorians were fisher-folk or lumberjacks, from Norway, Denmark, Sweden, and especially from Finland.

The first lumber mills came to Astoria in the 1840s, and industryt grew in the 1850s during the California gold rush. By the 1870s, Astoria became a center for the salmon fishing industry. Along with fishing came canneries. Most of Astoria's commerce took place in shops and canneries built on piers and wharves on the Columbia, rather than on dry land. In the late 19th Century, the canneries of Astoria put out nearly one million tons of canned salmon every year. Several small villages, such as Uppertown and Uniontown became incorporated into Astoria, while still maintaining their individual character. By 1900, Astoria was the second largest city in Oregon, with a population of over eight thousand people.

Fire had as much to do with the development of Astoria as the fishing or lumber mills. On 1 July 1883, almost all of Astoria's business district; stores, factories, mills and canneries were located on piers and pilings. On 2 July, someone threw a lit cigarette under the Clatsop mill, and within hours most of Astoria's business district burned to the water line. The surviving lumber mills quickly turned out enough rough lumber to rebuild. The city merchants installed fire hydrants and built some fire stations, while many canneries and businesses organized volunteer fire brigades to fight future fires. It was not enough.

Shortly after midnight on 7 December 1922, a small fire started in the basement of the Beehive Department Store. It may have been the Thiel Brothers pool hall, the fire spread so quickly, no one was sure. The firefighters pumped water directly out of the river to stop I. Around three in the morning, the city water mains burst, the city electricity failed, and the gas lines exploded. Some used dynamite to destroy buildings, creating firebreaks. That did not work either. By dawn, thirty city blocks were destroyed.

Astoria after the fire of 1922
Courtesy Compleat Photographer

As soon as the ashes cooled, the city began rebuilding. Most of the canneries were rebuilt on piers, as before. However, the city engineers dumped fill and rubble along the riverbank north of Exchange Street, creating dry land on what was a tidewater mark. Fortunately, the fire of 1922 did not climb the hills above Astoria, so many of the city's fine Victorian homes survived. The city rebuilt in a modern style, which was a mix of Art Deco and strangely, Greek Revival.

Being typical Astorians, they added some interesting Scandinavian designs to window shapes and building scrollwork. Most of the new buildings were built of brick and stone, with few remodels over the years. In the 1960s, many American cities rebuilt their downtown business district. The thrifty Astorians kept their buildings virtually unchanged. In the 1980s, as the local economy declined, they did not have the money to make major changes.

Because of the mix of old buildings, Astoria has an interesting look, which attracted many movie production companies. Perhaps the best known movie filmed in Astoria was *Goonies*, and the most recent was the horror film *The Ring II*. My personal favorite was *Kindergarten Cop*. With the fame of being a movie center came an increase in tourism, which Astoria embraced. Many old buildings have been refurbished as B&B's or restaurants and clubs.

Today Astoria has a population of around ten thousand. Many Astorians are descendents of some of the 19th Century settlers. Their family memories helped add details to the many historic haunts in Astoria. In recent years, newcomers have settled in Astoria. Fortunately, the older townsfolk have shared their history and traditions with them. As I researched this book, I could not tell the difference between old-timers and newcomers; they all love their town the same. The stories in this book are only a few of the many haunts in Astoria, helping document the history and heritage of this wonderful city.

Chapter 2

Ghost Ships and Sea Monsters

Some have called the mouth of the Columbia River, "the Graveyard of the Pacific." Since Robert Gray sailed across the sand bar in 1792, hundreds, even thousands of ships of various sizes sank there. With so many wrecks, many people have seen strange things, such as ghost ships over the years. Many Astorians may be reluctant to talk about these sightings, since they are related to family tragedies. Another reason may be that among sailors it is bad luck to talk about such things, which could foreshadow their own shipwreck. Even so, some stories were handed down the years of ships and sea monsters near Astoria.

Liisa Penner of Astoria provided many stories from the historic newspapers of the time, which I included in various places in this book. I divided the newspaper stories into paragraphs, and added some explanatory notes. Thanks, Liisa.

AN OPTICAL DELUSION

The Daily Morning Astorian June 22, 1878

There is just at this time a question being discussed at Fort Canby, as to whether the people are visited by a veritable ghost, or whether it is an optical delusion. If it is a ghost, it is a lively one; if an optical delusion, it is a success.

The whatever it is has appeared on several occasions of late, at various places on the cape in close proximity to the habitations of man, but never so closely to anybody as to the first officer of the steam launch *Katata* last Wednesday night. Capt. B.F. Stevens had gone ashore looking for a lost net belonging to Badollet & Co., and he left word with the first officer, Mr. Frank Hobson, that he would be back before bed time to be taken onboard. The *Katata* was anchored in the bay. Mr. Hobson, upon receiving the notice, went ashore, and while sitting on the dock, observed what he supposed to be Capt. Stevens coming down to go on board.

He spoke to him (or it), but receiving no answer, approached him (or it), when "it" very suddenly disappeared. Frank hadn't heard the ghost story and in fact he isn't very much on the run anyway, but thinking the sudden disappearance in the dark was a sort of a lark on the part of the object which he had taken to be a man, he looked around a little while, and finally observed "it" on the opposite side from where they had met before. Not wishing to be outdone, he approached "it" the second time, when "it" as mysteriously disappeared as before, but this time down under a bridge leading to the garrison.

As quick as thought, Frank leaped over the bank and followed "it" closely, but failing to find "it", sent sundry rocks after "it" into the darkness, until finally he seated himself on the side of the bridge and with a piece of the cape in each phist waited for "it" to appear again. "It" didn't come any more, but Capt. Stevens soon arrived and as he had heard of the ghost, was prepared to explain the apparition.

17

Frank says he is going to interview that ghost again the first chance he has, and find out what "it" represents. Since he has heard that it was a ghost, he thinks it must have been some relative of the Emperor Maximus or the veritable Gabara, who was brought out of Arabia as a ghost in the days of Claudius.

PHANTOM SHIP IN THE COLUMBIA RIVER
The Daily Morning Astorian, Jan. 28, 1881

Capt. E.D. Brock of the steamer Westport furnishes us with the particulars of some mysterious object seen on the Columbia River on Friday night last between 8 and 9 o'clock. What it was is yet a mystery to all who witnessed it, and that some light might be thrown on the subject we give this statement from Captain Brock, the truthfulness of which is vouched for by all on board.

He says, "I left Astoria for Westport via Hungry Harbor at 5 o'clock on Friday last. When I reached Pillar Rock, I saw two lights in range of Woody Island supposing them to be on shore, but as I neared Brookfield, the lights came along up the ship channel. I thought then that they were the lights of the bark *Webfoot.* I stopped at Brookfield to land freight during which time the object got as far as the Fisherton cannery.

When I started again I kept after it in the ship channel and constantly gained on it.

When I reached Bay View, I was within 200 yards of the object which was then on my port bow, and near shore when I remarked to the purser who was in the pilot house that it was about time the ship (as we supposed it was) was keeping out from shore. I put my wheel to port to give her more room. I gained all the time and when at Skamokawa, we were side by side not more than 200 feet apart.

I was just about to blow the whistle when the lights disappeared and nothing more could be seen. One was a bright light which appeared to be hung on the mast head; another was a red light appearing to be on the mizzen mast, and every few moments, we could see a number of small lights as they were on deck. The object before its disappearance was moving up river against a strong northeasterly breeze." The *Webfoot* did not leave Astoria until the following Sunday morning and no other vessel was in that part of the river at the time. What it was is a conundrum and could perhaps only be solved by the author of the Flying Dutchman.

The Peter Iredale

The *Peter Iredale* wrecked along the Oregon coast, in what is now Fort Stevens State Park, west of Warrenton. To my knowledge, the wreck is not haunted, but it is one of Oregon's most photographed seaside attractions. I felt I had to write about it and its ill fated sister ship, the *Ada Iredale*.

Peter Iredale was a British merchant who made his fortune in the coal industry. Iredale built a fleet of ships to transport his coal around the world. The *Peter Iredale* bridged the end of the era of sailing, but was still not completely part of the Industrial Age. Built in 1890 out of steel plates welded and riveted onto a steel frame, it weighted nearly 2,000 tons, and was two hundred seventy eight feet long. It did not use a propeller or paddle wheel but was a four masted sailing ship, called a Barquentine, or Barque.

The last leg of the *Peter Iredale's* final voyage began on 26 September 1906, in Santa Cruz, Mexico. She set out with a crew of twenty seven, and one thousand tons of ballast. The crew found two stowaways, who later wished they had stayed in Mexico. She was on her way to the Pacific Northwest to fill her hold with wheat, probably for transport to the Orient. The ship sailed for several weeks, approaching the mouth of the Columbia River. Early on the morning of 25 October, the lookout sighted the Tillamook Rock lighthouse. The captain adjusted course to pass close to the lighthouse, planning a course that would take them to the Columbia River Lightship.

The *Peter Iredale* found the lightship, but encountered heavy fog and lost her way. A pilot vessel, based out of Astoria, usually sailed those waters. Its experienced captain could have guided the *Peter Iredale* through the waters safely. Unfortunately, it was docked in Astoria, for repairs. The wind shifted to the west.

This change signaled the captain his ship's danger, from a combination of the wind, a northern ocean current, and the changing tide. These forces drove his ship toward the sand bar at the mouth of the Columbia. He attempted to steer away from the river, but the weather became worse, and the ship ran aground. The crew of the United States life saving station in Hammond reached the Peter Iredale, and rescued all aboard. A later Court of Inquiry found the captain and crew innocent of the loss of the *Peter Iredale*. The ship silted up in a storm, and eventually became buried.

In World War II, a Japanese submarine surfaced off Fort Stevens, and shelled the artillery emplacements. The next day, the U.S. Army set up a network of barbed wire along the beach, to repel an invasion. The *Peter Iredale* was included in this tangle foot. Periodically, high tides and other storms clear away the sand, exposing the rusting skeleton of the once proud ship.

The *Anne Iredale*

The *Anne Iredale,* named after Peter Iredale's daughter should be more interesting to readers than her sister ship. She was built in 1876, another sailing ship made of iron and steel. On 15 October 1876, the ship was carrying a load of coal in the South Pacific when the cargo caught fire. The crew abandoned her about 2,000 miles east of the Marquesas Islands. The ship drifted for eight months with her cargo still smoldering, before salvage crews boarded it, and sailed her to Tahiti. An American shipping company bought the ship, and changed her name. Perhaps they were sensitive to sailor's superstitions?

They renamed the ship the *Annie Thompson,* or the

Annie Johnson. As an upgrade, the owners installed a diesel engine and propeller in 1923. A few years later, a French shipping company bought the ship, and registered her out of Tahiti. The new owners changed her name to the *Bretagne*. In 1929, the *Bretagne* was sailing from Vancouver, British Columbia to Suva, in Fiji, with a load of canned salmon. She reached Cape Flattery, just outside of the Straight of Juan de Fuca, when she began taking on water in a heavy storm.

She sailed on for several days, until the situation became critical. It must have been agonizing for the crew, watching the water level rise over the days. Perhaps some of the crew knew the ships history. Maybe they muttered, and then openly talked about the *Anne Iredale* being jinxed. On 5 October, the ship was off the Oregon coast, when the situation became hopeless. The crew of seventeen, and the captain's family abandoned ship, where the *Whitney Olson* rescued them about fifteen miles south of the mouth of the Columbia.

The *Anne Iredale/Annie Johnson/Bretagne* drifted with the currents a few days before a U.S. Navy ship sunk her as a hazard to navigation. Perhaps the ship carried some memory of her previous abandonment and solo journey. Who knows how far she would have gone otherwise?

Claude (Seen along the mouth of the Columbia River)

In 1937 the crew of the Columbia River Lightship and her tender were treated to their first sight of a sea critter they named "Claude." According to L.A. Larson, the mate of the lightship, they saw a creature about 40 feet in length. A long, whip like tail took up a portion of its body. It had a long round body and a neck about eight feet long. He summed the whole creature as looking mean and snaky. He and the members of the crew studied the critter for several minutes with binoculars. Some crewmembers wanted to put out a boat and get close, but the officers refused to allow it.

In 1937, the Captain of the trawler *Viv* reported seeing a strange creature. It was long and sinewy, about 40 feet in length, and about four feet in diameter at its round middle. Unlike Larson's description, the *Viv's* Captain reported that this creature was covered with tan colored hair and had a head that was similar to an overgrown horse. Claude was seen several times over the next few years at the Columbia Bar and near Astoria.

Chris Anderson was the captain of the schooner *Arpo*. He and his crew saw Claude several times. They watched the predatory critter steal twenty pound fishes from their hooks. He described Claude as having a head like a camel with a bent snout. Claude's body was several feet long and covered with long gray fur. Claude was seen regularly at the mouth of the Columbia River until the 1950s when he either moved on or died. Or did he?

In 1989, Donald Riswick used to fish along the Shoo Fly drift, which is located east of Astoria. His gillnet boat was twenty eight foot long, with a powerful two hundred twenty five horse power engine. One September night he was trailing a net that was several hundred feet long and thirty four feet deep. He and his assistant had let their net sit for an hour and a half when they decided it was time to pull in their catch. The water at the drift was eighty feet deep. As they pulled in the net with a motorized winch they gathered a half dozen or so fish they had caught. They had only five hundred more feet of net to pull in when it snagged on something large and very heavy.

The ship had drifted with the current as they pulled in the net. When it began to unreel, the boat stopped it's downstream motion. They could have netted something stationary and the momentum of the boat was pulling against it. On the other hand, they could have hooked something that was swimming against the net and current. Riswick could not tell, as the bow of the boat began to sink. Riswick ran to the controls and opened up the throttle of the engine. They pulled free from whatever they had hooked. He could not understand, the net was only thirty four feet long, and the water was eighty feet deep. They could not have snagged the net on a piling or sunken obstacle. When Riswick pulled the net out of the water he found a hole big enough to drive a mini-van through.

He told his story to several other fishermen who suggested various theories about the strange event. Could he have snagged a sea lion, a whale, or one of the one ton sturgeon that have been spotted on the Oregon Coast?

Or could Claude still be swimming along the mouth of the Columbia River? Cryptozoologists search for and study animals that are supposed to be extinct, yet still exist. Some of them believe that creatures like Claude do exist, as a living relic of the times when massive sea creatures, not related to the whales swam the worlds oceans.

Chapter 3

Uppertown

UPPERTOWN FRIGHT
The Astoria Daily Budget March 29, 1894

The latest excitement in an Uppertown neighborhood is a haunted house. In the lonely hours of night, clumsy ghosts monkey around in the cat-loft, fall over chairs and smash dishes, when there is not any chairs and dishes there. Last night the occupants of the house called in a neighbor to help keep a watch for Mr. Ghosty, who made his presence felt by his usual antics at the hour of 12. The gentlemen on watch were armed to the teeth with guns, hatchets, and clubs and as soon as the racket started in the garret, they commenced to run a bluff on ghostly by pounding on the floor with their hatchets and hollering out that they would shoot.

After this break, the noise up stairs ceased and the next mysterious round was at the back door as if trying to enter. That settled it. The occupants proceeded without any ceremony to take their departure out of the front door. The affair is to be kept secret, and the Budget has promised to stand pat.

The Uppertown Firehouse Ghost (Astoria Children's Museum, and Firefighters Museum)

Following the disastrous fire which devastated Astoria in 1883, many neighborhoods, business and families set up volunteer fire departments. Most of the early fire stations were sheds with fire hose carts inside. Volunteer teams of men and women were responsible for pulling a large double-wheeled axle with 1,000 feet of heavy fire hose wrapped around it to the site of a fire. Once at the fire, they uncoiled the hose and attached it to fire hydrants, or started portable pumps, put in the river. These groups were called Muster Teams. There were several Women's Muster Team, and one year a woman's team won the Pacific Coast championships.

The Uppertown Fire Department benefited from the Volstead Act. Their fire station was built in 1896 as the North Pacific Brewery, which closed during Prohibition. It sat vacant for several years, until the city bought it, and converted the building into a fire station in 1930. The building remained a fire station until 1960, and re-opened as a museum in 1990.

While it was a fire station, fire engines were parked

on the ground floor and the firefighter's rooms were on the second floor. The third floor was used as a combination storage facility and youth club. Dick Williams worked as a firefighter for 33 years. He and other firefighters were aware something was strange about the third floor. Odd things did not happen every night, but happened weekly or monthly. It usually sounded like things being dragged across the floor. Sometimes the ghost came down to their quarters on the second floor.

Williams and fellow firefighter Sid Larsen spent many nights in the firehouse. A large calendar hung on the wall of the dayroom. When people walked passed the calendar it would sometimes pull away from the wall, toward the person walking by. Many times in the middle of the night, the doors on the fire crew's equipment lockers rattled and shook. Sometimes the noises were loud enough to awaken the firefighters. They tried to find the person who did it, but never could. One night, Sid Larsen woke up in the middle of the night and saw someone in his room. He called to Dick Williams. He said there was someone standing over his bed. The two of them searched the building but could find no intruder.

When the firehouse closed, gear was stored there. To prevent any damage from cold or moisture, the heating system had to be maintained. A work crew checked the old furnace every afternoon. Like the firefighters, several times, they returned and reported strange noises on the third floor. Though they never found anyone in the building.

In 2006, I spoke with Martha, with the Clatsop County Historical Society, which runs the Firefighter's Museum. She told me that another volunteer, Tom, used to be the primary caretaker there. He worked there for several years, and always talked about the ghosts. He never saw anything, but said he heard things. He was more than happy to take visitors, sit them down and talk for several minutes about ghosts, the paranormal, existentialism, and many other things. Unfortunately, Tom has moved on, and I did not have a chance to speak with him.

Martha had one odd, but perhaps not a ghostly experience once. One day she was in the museum near the entrance, waiting for a tour group to come in. To the best of her knowledge, she was alone in the building. As she waited, Martha became aware of the sound of heavy footsteps walking across the ceiling above her. She thought someone was on the second floor. She went to the foot of the stairs, and yelled, "Hello, is there someone there?"

There was no answer. She could not go to investigate. Although Martha did not believe in ghosts, she might have been afraid of an intruder. She remembered later that the roof above her was the rooftop of the building. The second and third stories were built at the other end of the building. Was someone walking across the roof, playing a joke on her? How did they get on the roof then? How did they get off later?

One fixture in all fire stations is the brass pole firefighters slide down to get to the engines. When I visited the museum, a staff member pointed out the sealed opening around the brass pole. Tradition has it that a firefighter who used to sleepwalk fell through the hole and died. His ghost is supposed to haunt this building. This may be mixed up with the story of Paul Marion, a firefighter who worked out of the old fire station at 4th and Astor Street. In 1928, he fell down the brass pole hole at his station and died.

In the summer of 2006, the Advanced Ghost Hunters of Seattle and Tacoma, (AGHOST,) visited the firefighters museum. Some ghost hunters divide hauntings into different categories. Many houses are haunted by spirits who are aware they are dead, but who remain behind. Other hauntings are associated with memories of events that happened in a building, or are attached to objects. There is no real intelligence behind these hauntings. Jody, one of their intuitive, or psychic members felt several residual memories in the place. They could have been attached to the items on display, but no actual ghosts. Jody may have encountered an entity in the kitchen space, she received impressions of several names that might have been local folks, but received no confirmation from local researchers

As she walked up the stairs, to the second floor, she felt an odd pain in her leg. She believed that in the past, a man who had lost a leg in some kind of accident used to walk up the stairs. Every time he did, he had a spasm of pain, when he reached that spot. When she talked with one of the volunteers, he told her that he also had strange pains on that very spot.

Once she reached the second floor, she felt a kind of energy source that was not human. It was not a remnant memory either. It had been like a "paranormal volcano" in the past, but it had lost most of it's energy. It was like an extinct cinder cone, but reflected some energy, perhaps from the daycare located on the second floor. In addition, she felt drawn to the equipment lockers near the firefighters quarters. She felt that although this was not a negative energy, she did not like it. This was the same area where firefighters had reported their apparitions in the past. What else was happening there? Only time will tell.

The Sailor in a Slicker (Private residence on Leif Eriksson Drive)

I began this book in the summer of 2006, by contacting my friend Regina, who worked at the Astoria-Hammond Chamber of Commerce. She told me that some of her coworkers had strange experiences, and introduced me to Barb, one of their long time volunteers. Barb moved to the Astoria area in the early 1990s and bought a house on Leif Erikson Boulevard. The house was built in the late 1800s, a few miles east of Uppertown and Astoria proper. Sailors who docked their ships on the nearby wharves built this house and those around it. Barb moved into her house in

October, on a dark and stormy day.

Barb and her husband had already moved in most of their boxes when she noticed an unusual sight. She walked into the dining room, and saw a man standing there, wearing a rain slicker. He looked at her, walked into the living room, and disappeared. The man was taller than Barb, thin, with a beard. When Barb saw the man, she did not feel frightened; instead she felt a peaceful sensation, like the man was welcoming them to the house.

Sometime later, Barb's husband Steve was watching television when he looked down the hallway and saw a man wearing a green slicker and hat watching him. After a second, the man disappeared.

Although sightings were rare, the man was most active in the fall. In the weeks after they moved in, Barb and Steve both smelled pipe smoke, even though no one in the house smoked one. At first Steve assumed that it was somehow an odor left by previous residents. It continued for some time, past the time when it should have faded away. Most of the time, they smelled the smoke upstairs. It eventually faded, but reoccurred at times, generally when they had guests.

A few years after they moved in, Barb and Steve were sitting in the living room watching television. She sat at one end of the room, where she looked out the window, at the sea. Steve sat at the other end of the room, with one foot on the coffee table, talking to Barb. It was quiet and peaceful, and neither of them was thinking of a ghost. Suddenly, Steve felt someone rub his back. He jumped up and turned round, looking for the masseuse. No one was there. Although it was a surprise, Steve did not feel any menace in this disembodied touch. Later he felt it was more like a friend touching another in a gesture of fellowship.

In addition to incidents within the house, this ghost occasionally followed Barb out to the garden. She told me that several times, someone gently swatted her on the behind, as she bent over her planting beds. When this happened, she always straightened up, looked around, and has never seen anyone. It has never been hard enough to leave a handprint.

Barb has relatives who will not stay overnight. The first time Barb's sister Jane stayed overnight, she slept in the living room. Barb had a dinosaur puppet, which she placed on her television. In the middle of the night, it somehow "fell" off the table onto her sister. This fall was over a distance of eight feet.

Guests have heard tapping on windows at night. Towels have moved from the bathroom, only to be found somewhere else in the house. Every now and then, the dogs would look up at an unseen guest. The number of incidents went down over time, as though the spirit gathered energy, waiting for someone new to stay at the house.

After my first talk with Barb, I visited her, Steve and their guest, Kelsey at their house. Kelsey worked for as an intern for the Department of Fish and Wildlife. When she knew she was coming to Astoria, Kelsey contacted the Chamber of Commerce, looking for a place to stay. Barbara worked there, and after exchanging some emails offered to let Kelsey stay there. She moved into an upstairs bedroom in May, and immediately noticed a few things that seemed odd, but she did not think they were ghostly.

That is, until July, when Barb mentioned that house was haunted. Barb told Kelsey about the strong smell of pipe tobacco. When she was in her room, Kelsey smelled pipe tobacco several times when she first moved in. It usually happened in the early evenings, and on overcast nights. She always assumed Steve was smoking a pipe in his upstairs office. Barb told her that Steve did not smoke a pipe. I asked them why they were so calm about the whole thing. Barb pointed out other people could afford to be frightened. They could just leave and go home. Steve and Barb lived in the house, and could not let themselves be frightened by any strange experiences. Therefore, they just got along.

Chapter 4

Astoria and Uniontown

The Flavel House

I cannot describe the haunting of the Flavel House without describing the Flavel family. Like many of the Pacific Northwest's *nouveau riche,* they were an interesting group. Sometimes this was good; sometimes it was a bad thing.

Where Captain George Flavel was born is something of a mystery. It could have been Ireland, Virginia, or New

Jersey. He did say he was born in 1823, and historic records show that he became a member of the Oddfellows in 1846, shortly before he sailed from Norfolk, Virginia to the West Coast. Captain Flavel commanded the *John Petty* on a voyage to San Francisco, arriving there in August 1849. He later sailed to Portland, in what was the Oregon Territory, where he unloaded his cargo.

Over the next year or so, Captain Flavel sailed back and forth along the coast. He saw business possibilities in the growing town of Astoria. In 1850, he applied for a license to act as a ship pilot; a special navigator who boarded ships, guiding them through treacherous waters. In addition to guiding ships across the sand bars at the mouth of the Columbia, Captain Flavel guided ships up the Columbia and Willamette Rivers. Captain Flavel was not the first river pilot, but he was a combination of the best and luckiest.

At first, Captain Flavel guided all the ships, first by approaching on a dug out canoe, and climbing aboard on ropes. Soon he owned several pilot boats, maneuverable little vessels that guided ships around the many sand bars. Pilots who worked for Flavel commanded each boat, allowing him to stop that dangerous work, to concentrate on other projects. Even though he had rivals, most acknowledged that Flavel got what he had by good business, not through shady dealings. Captain Flavel owned wharves, warehouses, a small fleet of sailing ships, and had large land holdings in Clatsop County. For many years, he commanded one of these ships, sailing between San Francisco and Portland. San Francisco became a second home city for Captain Flavel and his family.

His wife, Mary Boelling, was born in 1839, the child of German immigrants, who had traveled along the Oregon Trail in 1847. Mary's father Conrad, spent some time in California in search of gold, while the family moved to Astoria in 1848. Conrad returned to his family in 1849, with $1,500, and built a hotel in Astoria. George Flavel stayed at their hotel when he was in Astoria. In 1854, the Boellings agreed to have their fourteen year old Mary marry thirty year old Captain Flavel. Although this arranged marriage would be illegal today, it was common in the 19th Century, and George and Mary made it work.

They had three children, George Conrad, born in 1856, Nellie, born in 1857, and Katie, born in 1864. The Flavel girls benefited from the tutors their parents hired in San Francisco, and later in Europe. Nellie, a talented pianist, also played the organ and violin. Katie Flavel was a cultured soprano, and sang at the professional level.

In addition to their musical talents, Nellie and Katie both spoke several languages, and held discussions on subjects of science and philosophy. They never married, but were content to live with their parents, and travel across the world. Most of what we know of the Flavel family comes from the diaries of the Flavel sisters.

George Conrad Flavel seems disconnected from the rest of the family. As a child, his mother described him as fat and impudent. The family sent him to a military academy in San Francisco when he was older. Later he boarded the ship *Whistler*, and traveled the world for several years before returning to Astoria. Some Astorians suggest that Captain Flavel was so upset at his unruly son that he had a friendly ship captain kidnap the boy for his own good.

When George Conrad returned to Astoria, he worked in many of his father's businesses. He also married a local woman, and in time began a family of his own. Captain Flavel eased into retirement in the 1880s, gradually turning over business to his son. One of Captain Flavel's retirement projects was his fine mansion. By that time, George Conrad and his new family were established in their own home. I had not heard of whether he played any musical instruments or was a talented singer. He seems to have spent his later adult life as a solid banker and business manager, despite his earlier, wild youth. He died in 1923, of bronchial pneumonia.

Captain George Flavel's house was meant to be a cultured residence for his family as well as a showplace for Captain Flavel's political life. German born architect Carl Leick designed the mansion, relying on the standard elements of Queen Anne architecture, an asymmetrical floor plan, including an octagonal tower, decorative shingles, and stained glass. He added elements of a short lived style called Western Stick, which included square sided bay windows, side brackets, and square porch supports.

Construction lasted from 1884 to 1886. The house had over 11,000 square feet of space in two main stories and an unfinished attic. The ground floor had fourteen foot high ceilings, and the second floor ceilings were thirteen feet high. When the Flavels lived in the house, the basement had a dirt floor, which was replaced by a concrete foundation.

The first floor had public rooms off a central hallway. There was a formal parlor, and library on the right, with a music room and dining room on the left. The kitchen and stairs to the second floor were at the end of the hallway. Like many grand houses, there was a second, servant's stair in the back of the house, in the kitchen. On the second floor were several bedrooms, and the bathroom. Each of the Flavels, the Captain, his wife Mary, and their daughters Nellie and Katie had their own rooms. The bathroom had a flush toilet and a small metal bathtub. Just off the stairway, was a guest bedroom, and another small, multipurpose room. The servant stairs continued on to the attic.

Captain Flavel enjoyed his dream mansion for less than a decade, dying there in 1893, while his wife and daughters were traveling on the east coast. Over the next forty one years, his wife and daughters traveled across the world, but always returned to Astoria. Nellie was the longest lived of the trio, dying in 1933. After she died, Patricia Jean Flavel, great granddaughter of Captain George Flavel donated the house to the city of Astoria. It was a long time and many changes took place until it became a museum and interpretive center.

In 1951, the Clatsop County Historical Society turned the house into a museum. They maintain a gift shop, and interpretive center in the ground floor of the Carriage House, and have offices on the second floor. After Nellie's death, many of the original Flavel furniture was removed. The Flavel family sold it or gave it away to friends. In the last decades, some townsfolk have donated or sold many of these items to the historical society, who returned them to the house.

Before visiting the Flavel house, I did some quick searching for ghost stories on the Internet. There was not much definite, other than reports of lights being turned off when left on by caretakers, or phones ringing when not plugged in, and drapes closing or opening by themselves.

The people at the Clatsop County Historical Society were very helpful in giving me information about the Flavel Family, their house, and a few of their own ghost stories. Some of them were a bit skeptical about ghosts, but I appreciated their cooperation. I owe particular thanks to Martha, Mac, and Steve, who had not had anything happen to them, but shared incidents that other people had reported to them.

The Music Room

Sharon worked as a volunteer at the house for five years. As the docent (caretaker,) she used to sit in the main hallway, near the entrance. Opposite her chair was the music room. Although there was a formal parlor, Katie and Nellie spent most of their mornings in the music room, waiting to receive visitors, and practicing their music. In the evenings, they entertained visitors with song and sound. Like most of the rooms, the furnishings were a mix of original Flavel furniture, and period pieces from elsewhere. When Sharon was there, she noticed a large music box in the music room.

On stormy days, as it got dark, Sharon sometimes heard the music box playing on its own. The first time this happened, she investigated and found that the doorway was roped off and the room was empty. The music box had a large, heavy lid, which had to be lifted to start the mechanism.

Her memory was pretty good, and she did not remember hearing or seeing anyone enter the music room, lift the lid, start the music box, lower the lid, and creep out. Sharon spoke with some of the other volunteers, and they told her they had heard it play sometimes, usually before a storm. When I visited in July 2006, I asked after the music box. The volunteers recalled that there had been one in the music room, however, no one seemed sure where it went.

I spoke with another volunteer; Joan who shared her experience. In 2005, her son, his wife, and their children came to Astoria for a visit. She took them on a tour of the house, finishing in time to close up the house for the day. They paused for a while outside before going home. Her son and husband took several pictures of the house from different angles, each with their own digital cameras. When they got home, her son downloaded his pictures to their computer. They noticed something strange in one of the music room windows.

They saw fuzzy images of what they believed to be three women standing there, looking outside. Her husband downloaded his pictures next. He also had a picture of the three women standing at the window. On close examination, the women were wearing old-fashioned clothing. Were the Flavel women looking out the window, wishing them a good evening? She offered to show me the pictures on my next visit. Unfortunately, we never reconnected, and I missed seeing the ghostly ladies.

Captain Flavel's Bedroom

Most of the furniture in Captain Flavel's room is original. His bed was a recent acquisition, purchased at an auction a year or two ago. One of the people who bid on the bed told me that there was a bullet hole in the headboard. When I visited, I tried checking for it, but got yelled at, so I do not recommend checking yourself. If there is one, I am sure there is a story to tell.

Three or four years ago, a woman came to tour the house, near closing time. She identified herself as a psychic and requested permission to walk the house, after they closed. The docent told her it was fine, and after closing let her walk around the building. The woman approached Captain Flavel's bedroom, and walked inside. She paused just inside the threshold, and turned to the docent, saying, "this, this is the center of all evil in the house!"

A few years later, as part of a Halloween newspaper article, the same docent stayed overnight in the house with a reporter from the *Daily Astorian*. He made sure to sleep on the evil spot, and unfortunately, (for this book,) nothing bad happened.

One of the volunteers told Martha a story, which took place before 2002, when the gift shop opened in the carriage house. In those days, the docent sat at a desk in the house, at the foot of the grand staircase, selling tickets. A man the docent described as "perfectly normal," came tearing down the staircase, white as a sheet, very upset. The man said he saw Captain Flavel in his bedroom. He saw Captain Flavel's figure, standing there for a few seconds, looking at him. Then Captain Flavel crumbled to the floor, and disappeared. It seemed like he fell through, or sank through the floor.

I spoke with a woman who worked as a housekeeper at the Flavel House, who I will call Mary. On her first day, Mary cleaned the Captain's bedroom. Mary was not alone in the building, but as far as she knew, she was the only one on the second floor. She was vacuuming the carpet, when the machine suddenly cut out.

When she checked the vacuum, and plug in, she found that the electrical cord was unplugged. she plugged it back in, and went on cleaning. A minute or so later, it was unplugged again. Mary figured that some of the other volunteers were playing tricks on her, and yelled for them to stop. A quick check of the second floor showed Mary that she was alone.   Mary told me that something similar happened a few more times. She felt that Captain Flavel was just trying to be playful.

In addition to Captain Flavel dying in his room, Katie died there in August, 1910 of what they called, inanition due to neuritis. Some people suggest that her lingering illness was multiple sclerosis, or rheumatoid arthritis. Mary Flavel died in her bedroom, after a long illness, in 1928. Nellie did not die at home, but had of a heart attack, while visiting relatives in New York state in 1933.

Another testament to the rough and ready days of Astoria's past were the security doors the Flavel women installed on the second floor, after the Captain's death. The caretakers keep these doors open now. They appear to be decorative, but are functional. They are wooden, and are heavily decorated, but go from floor to ceiling. There were brackets, where a board could be dropped, to barricade the door shut, if an intruder managed to pick the locking bolt from the outside. Some friends remember Nellie locking the doors most nights, for fear of robbers.

The Attic and Tower

Laurie worked at the Chamber of Commerce for several years, and received a VIP tour of the Flavel house. In the days when the house was built, servants usually lived in small nooks in the attic. The attic spaces were drafty and drab then, and today. Most of the Flavel servants lived locally, and worked as day servants.

Captain Flavel went up there to climb to the top of the tower to survey the Columbia River and his domain. The stairs are about six feet wide as they begin the climb up the tower. They narrow to about eighteen inches as they end at the observation window. Flavel climbed these stairs so often his hand polished the wooden handrail lining the stairs. Laurie tried following his footsteps.

Laurie made it most of the way up these stairs before she turned back. She admits that she had a bit of claustrophobia, but she also felt something telling her not to go up to the top of the stairs. She had no explanation of what was up there, but was curious about what other people felt. I climbed the stairs myself, and did not notice anything strange. However, the way the stairs narrow, and the cobwebs would bother anyone with a touch of claustrophobia.

The Eagles Lodge

As this book went to print, the Astoria Eagles Lodge was vacant, perhaps awaiting a makeover and change in venue. I hope the ghosts and whatever else is there will remain. Sharon told me about two of her friends who worked there. They sometimes heard sounds coming from the attic, like footsteps. Whenever they investigated, they found everything in its place, and no animals or people who could have made the noise.

They told Sharon about this when she began bartending there. Before Sharon started work, someone found mice in the basement. The managers blocked up the entrances, and had exterminators kill the vermin. While Sharon worked there, the health inspectors visited several times, and confirmed there were not mice or rats in the building. Sharon tended bar from noon to nine Even so, she heard noises coming from the attic above her. This happened sporadically the seven months she worked there.

One night the noises were very loud, and Sharon warned who or whatever was above, "I've got a gun, and I've got a bottle handy down here. Which one do you want to be hit with first!?!"

The noises stopped. Sharon lied; she did not have a gun, but she did have a bottle. This happened most of the time when she was alone in the building. However Sharon was determined not to be chased out. She told me that people backed away when she took a stand. Strangely, after talking to her, it is not difficult for me to imagine five foot tall Sharon scaring a ghost, empty bottle in hand.

Sharon was not the only one to hear the noise. Her friend Yvonne heard it the attic noises sometimes, even when her co-worker did not. Yvonne was glad when Sharon began working, because Sharon was a fellow witness, rather than Yvonne being the only "one crazy."

The Liberty Theater

The Liberty Theater owes its existence to the tragic fire of 1922. Before the fire, the Weinhart Astoria Hotel stood on part of the theater site. It was billed as a "modern fireproof hotel" of brick and steel. No one expected the destructive heat of the fire, to ignite these fire resistant materials. What the fire did not destroy, the firefighters finished. Many buildings were blown up with dynamite to create firebreaks. Thirty city blocks were destroyed. After the fire, the city began rebuilding itself.

To increase public confidence, public buildings like stores and theaters were a priority. In 1923, Jensen and Von Herberg built a six hundred seat theater at 11th and Exchange street. This was the first Liberty Theater. Although the new theater included an organ, electric lights, and stained glass, it was not big enough. In 1924, investors purchased land at 12th and Commercial Street. They wanted a theater that could seat one thousand people, with room for several stores, and offices, and restaurants.

Architects Bennes and Herzog designed the next Liberty Theater. The overall theme was what they called Romanesque, with light Italianate. This may be true, but there were other different elements, such as the Hacienda style, tiled roof, Greek Columns, and the Chinese paper and silk chandelier in the auditorium. The principal interior designs were a series of Venetian inspired paintings done by eclectic artist Joseph Knowles.

Knowles became a national celebrity in 1913, when he lived for two months in the woods of Maine, wearing nothing but a jockstrap. (This was probably in the summer. I hope.) He wrote a book of his experiences, which sold 30,000 copies. Knowles married Marian Humphries, and they settled in a shack built of driftwood near Long Beach, Washington, in 1917. He celebrity status brought him occasional work as an artist and author.

Knowles competed for the prize of providing the master painting plans for the Venetian designs of the new Liberty Theater. That was quite a task, since Knowles had never been to Venice before. Still, in six weeks he gave the architects twelve large canvases detailing stylized Venetian waterways. Many of the local sailors undoubtedly recognized some of the views as the Columbia River, with gondolas instead of their fishing boats.

Weinhart Hotel after the fire.
Courtesy of Compleat Photographer

The new Liberty Theater was the gem of Astoria's entertainment scene. At first patrons watched silent movies and vaudeville performers. They continued to come after movies became talkies, and vaudeville faded away. They packed the theater in World

War II to watch newsreels, and buy War Bonds, sold by people like Jack Dempsey. In addition to movies and the businesses on the first floor, most of the boys and girls in Astoria learned to dance at a second floor studio. Teachers had to make sure that the kids did not glance across the street into some of the open windows of the Hotel Elliott, and get another kind of education.

Unfortunately, the Liberty Theater suffered the same fate as many other grand theaters. In the 1950s, Americans began to stay at home at night to watch television. With fewer patrons, maintenance was not done, and the theater became run down. In the 1990s, the owners turned the one screen theater into a tri-plex. Eventually the theater closed. Fortunately, in 1998 the Liberty Restoration non-profit group bought it. Over the years, they finished several restoration projects. The eight foot tall, Chinese lantern style chandelier made of paper and cotton cost over $100,000 to restore.

While researching this book, I met with Rosemary

and Larry at the Liberty Theater. They took me on a tour of the recently restored vaudeville house in 2006. Neither of them have had anything spooky or paranormal happen to them, though they get   phone calls and emails about ghosts at the Liberty Theater. I promised I would help them settle some of the urban myths surrounding the place.

The first book I know of which mentions any haunts at the Liberty Theater was *Twilight Visitors*, (written by Sharon Gill and Dave Oester,) in 1995. The authors mention three ghosts in the Liberty, Lily, Paul, and Mary. Paul and Mary are tied together. Mary was a prostitute, and Paul was her pimp. When Mary wanted to quit, Paul followed her into the second floor ladies bathroom, grabbed her, and threw her off the upper balcony area. Mary was reported in the balcony and the restroom, where she was seen looking outward, from the mirror. Paul wandered the building, and basement. According to their informants, Lily was watching a movie, and was killed by an angry lover, who slit her throat. She supposedly haunts the seat where she died.

After *Twilight Visitors* was published, many people investigated the story. I visited Astoria in 1998, and spoke to Liisa Penner of the Clatsop County Historical Society. She told me that the *Daily Astorian* newspaper never mentions anyone being killed at the Liberty Theater.

Larry usually worked late at night, when the building was very quiet. The way the theater was built, if someone flushed a toilet, it could be heard across the building. One night he was working late at night and was startled to hear the sound of a coast guard cutter PA system calling out orders four blocks away. The sound had blasted through the ventilation system, into the projection booth. Several people have told me that there was more than one Liberty Theater.

It is possible that some events happening at an earlier theater are now retold as happening in the current one. At the other Liberty, a ticket taker fell from the balcony, and was injured or killed. Perhaps this accounts for some of the stories, which amount almost to an urban legend. Despite this, there are people at the current Liberty Theater, with stories of their own.

Rosemary told me that in October 2005 the cleaning woman said she did not want to be in the building alone. She told Rosemary that when she was in the upstairs ladies bathroom, the water faucets would turn on by themselves. At other times, her cleaning cart would move when she left it unattended for a few minutes. I spoke with two women, Brenda and Anna, who went to the theater before the renovation. They both reported feeling something "eerie." One of them said she had a dream that she went to the Liberty Theater, walked up to the women's bathroom and opened the door. When she did, a white light nearly blinded her; there was so much energy.

Investigators from AGHOST have visited the Liberty many times, and had many intriguing incidents. So many, that it would take a whole volume to discuss. One interesting incident happened to Stephanie and Ross, in the basement. Stephanie, a psychic tried to tune in on any paranormal entities. She developed a headache, and said something was putting pressure on her. Ross was filming her, and was shocked when a gray shape stepped in front of the camera. It stopped for a few seconds, as if it wanted its picture taken. After a few frames, it passed on, into the shadows. Sometime later, another less defined shape moved by the camera lens very quickly. Some people watching the tape on replay claim they even heard a whooshing sound.

Ross played an audio clip that another investigator gave him. On the recording, the investigator asked the spirit if it knew why it was there. Another voice, distinctly feminine replied. Investigations continue, though I ask readers not to pester the managers for tours.

Mary's Mirror

The strangest story about Mary, was that she appeared in the mirror, in the women's bathroom, as if she was standing behind the patron. When the person turned around, there was no one there. Since the remodel, workers took down the old mirror and replaced it with a new one. Rosemary told me that they hung the old one in her office. Rosemary told Mary she was welcome to appear in the mirror, as long as she did not frighten anyone. Rosemary never saw anyone.

While we doing our walkthrough, after my interview Larry told her that she had the wrong mirror, the original one was in storage. I wonder if they have had time to change the mirrors, and if anything has happened.

Ghostly Workmen?

Sharon lived two blocks from Liberty Theater. She did not drive a car, so she has seen many unusual things as she walked around town. Some time before the remodel of the Liberty Theater, she was walking from her job to her apartment building. It was in early fall, and getting dark. There was a street light on, and she looked through a glass door or window, inside the theater lobby. She saw two men bending over something. One man was very tall, wearing bib overall, and a country style hat. The other man was older, and shorter. At first, she thought they were intruders. She watched them carefully, to memorize features, so she could report them to the police.

After several minutes, the tall man turned around and saw her, and the he and Sharon locked eyes. The man was clean shaven, but looked like a rough farmer. His overalls were solid blue. It seemed to Sharon they stood there for several minutes, though it may have been only seconds. Then both men disappeared. These days, she does not walk by the Liberty Theater at night unless she knows there are other people around.

The Owens Adair Apartments

Sharon lived in the Owens-Adair Apartments. A lot of Astoria's history is piled under the foundations of this building. The original Fort Astoria was built not too far away, and a replica bastion stands across the street. The Providence Sisters of Charity set up a hospital on this site in 1889. In 1931, the current building was constructed as the St Mary's hospital. In 1981, the building was remodeled and turned into apartments for the elderly, and renamed the Owens-Adair Apartments.

Sharon moved into her apartment a few years ago, and her mother has moved in with her. This is usually not unusual, except her mother moved in, **after** her death in 2002. For most people, the thought of a deceased loved one watching over them would be comforting. For Sharon and her brother James, Mom was more of a pain than a comfort. They never got along, because her mother did not like girls (daughters). Sharon felt that the haunting was a last malicious act on the part of her mother. She said, "I thought once I got rid of her, I got rid of her."

Strange things began happening a few months after James moved in with her, in 2003. Several times when Sharon sat on the sofa, she felt it move under her, even when she was sitting quietly. Sharon also started hearing the sound of an unseen person walking down the hallway, into the kitchen. James sometimes went into his room at night, only to return to the living room a few minutes later asking, "did you call me?"

Of course, she had not. He was firm; he had heard a woman's voice calling him. She always told him, it was not her. Sharon speculated that the voice was her mother, calling to her favorite son. Hoping it was not the spirit of her dead mother; Sharon suggested that the ghost came from the days when her apartment was a hospital room. Other residents told Sharon that they felt presences in their rooms. After all, some hospital patients died, as well as elderly tenants. Like whatever existed in the basement.

Sharon never left her apartment after 10 at night. She did once, to drop off her garbage. The garbage drop off point was in a room that tenants were not allowed to use for storage. That night she went to the drop off point and heard something like heavy breathing in the room with her. She looked around, but did not see anything there. She hurried back up the stairs. She did not want to take the elevator, lest whatever IT was get in with her.

At the other end of the garbage drop off room, there was a door leading into another room. It was always locked. Someone told her that when St Mary's had been a hospital, the locked room was used as a morgue or embalming room. The manager offered her the locked room for her storage. As crowded as her apartment may become, I am sure that Sharon will never use this room.

The Hotel Elliott

I spoke with Chester Trabucco about the history of the Hotel Elliott. Although Chester was not born in Astoria, he moved there when he was two years old and has a long history of working in and around the hotel. He learned the history of the building from the granddaughter of the Jeremiah Elliott, who the hotel was named after. Jeremiah Elliott worked as a manager for a retail corporation in the early 20th Century, probably J. C. Penny. The job eventually took him to the Pacific Northwest, where he became angry after being passed over for promotion. He quit the corporate world and followed his dream of owning and running a hotel. His search for a new property took him to Astoria, shortly after the fire of 1922.

The Elliott Hotel was under construction at the time, and originally named the Niemi Hotel, a common Finnish name. Mr. Elliott started with a lease, but eventually bought the property. The construction workers who helped rebuild

Astoria were probably the hotels first customers. Like many of the post-fire buildings, the buildings were finished as soon as possible, and they added luxury features later. The hotel opened in 1924, with 68 rooms. It was supposed to be a four story building, but a fifth story was added during construction. The lobby was quite small, like many hotels of the time; the ground floor of the Elliott included a restaurant, and several retailers. The basement was not used by customers.

The Elliot family used the hotel basement for their own purposes. Jeremiah Elliott had several children. His son John was married, and his daughter married a business associate named Clarence Short. They all lived in the hotel together. Part of the basement under the sidewalk was outfitted as a combination living room, kitchen, and household working space.

Apparently, Jeremiah's daughter and daughter-in-law did not get along. They so detested each other that they had identical appliances, such as stoves, refrigerators and dishes,

rather than sharing. Most of the light came from the light wells imbedded in the sidewalk above, and dim floor lamps near the living room couch. It was a dreary place, which the family rarely left, except for an annual trip to Portland. They lived with this arrangement for several decades.

Although they spent their days in the basement, the family slept in rooms on the fifth floor. They had four bedrooms, which the recent renovation combined into three rooms, as part of the Presidential Suite. Many of the Elliott's died there. Jeremiah Elliott's wife was in a coma toward the end of her life. . She died there, after seven years of care. Her bed was located on the spot where the living room couch now sits. Jeremiah's daughter died of a heart attack in what is now the Presidential Suite bathroom.

John Elliott eventually took over the hotel, and ran it into debt, and lost it in 1969. The family moved to what is now the Franklin Street Bed and breakfast. Jeremiah was an invalid by that time and his living room had a clear view of the hotel he owned for over forty years. He died soon after the move. The hotel had two owners from 1969 through 1999. It began a slow decline into what some called a fleabag hotel. This time coincided with a decline in people wanting to stay at hotels, in favor of motor inns and motels. These years also saw the economy of Astoria fail, as timber and fishing revenues declined. It was during this time that Chester became familiar with the Hotel Elliott

From 1974 to 1979, Chester's first *adult* job was carpet cleaning in and around Astoria. He used the Hotel Elliott as a message center. He went there several times a day, to pick up any assignments. He told me that he has always been an inquisitive person. However, there was something about the look and feel of the hotel at that time. It was so foreboding, that he never asked for a tour of the building. He was not the only one.

I spoke with several of the hotel employees. One of the women at the front desk told me that her mother had been a resident in the 1990s. She and her friends used to walk through the lobby and up the stairs to her mother's room. It was not a nice trip. She remembered the old vending machine in one corner, the dirty floors, and the old man who always sat in the lobby, as if he had no place to go.

In 1999, Chester returned to the Elliott, this time to renovate and restore it. They turned it into a wonderful luxury hotel, with some old fashioned touches. During the 2003 remodel, they found many ornate light fixtures, at odds with the larger number of utilitarian fixtures. The lobby had a lot of intricate woodwork and molding. This was repeated on the second floor, but visitors notice that the woodwork becomes less fancy as they go up to the other floors. Perhaps when the hotel budget got smaller as the building work continued, they used whatever materials were cheapest at the time. Chester saved some vestiges from the days when the hotel was used by low income residents. Many of the stairwells are decorated with folk art painted by these guests.

During renovation, Chester came in late one night. He went to the basement and spoke with a carpenter, who was working late. Suddenly there was a loud crash, and the building shook. It was obvious the sound came from inside the hotel. The next morning, they looked around but did not find anything broken or fallen that could have made that size of a disturbance.

The Opening Days

Jody was not born in Astoria. As a relative Captain William Clark, Jody felt that his moving to Astoria was a matter of fate. He left Portland during the dot.com crash in 2001, and moved to Astoria. He put on his best suit, and walked the streets looking for work. He walked by the front door of the Hotel Elliott, and saw a "Help Wanted" sign. He thought the hotel looked like a dive, but he needed work. He walked inside, and was treated to a tour of the building. After the tour, he asked for a job, and Chester hired him.

Jody was the first night auditor when they opened, in the middle of the remodel. They had two guests that night. It was a good thing, since they only had four rooms available. Jody heard rumors that the place was haunted, but he did not let it worry him. Four months later, the lobby was finished, as were the second through fourth floors. Unfortunately, the fifth floor was not completed, and Jody had to make regular inspections of the top floor for safety's sake.

Between fire checks, Jody stayed at the front desk doing paperwork. One night, he bent under the front desk, searching one of the drawers to find something. When he straightened up, Jody saw a man sitting in a chair near the front door. The chair faced the bank, outside, and Jody saw the man's profile quite clearly. He was bald with glasses, and wore a black suit with a bow tie. Oh, and he was transparent.

The man stood up and faced Jody, made eye contact, then looked toward the bank and disappeared. Jody looked through several picture albums of past owners and employees. He thought the man resembled the original owner, Jeremiah Elliott. Jody talked to one of the Elliott family descendents. Based on his description, the relative guessed that the man was Jeremiah's brother. According to her, this brother was a bit odd. When not working, he spent his time in the lobby, sitting in a chair by the entrance looking outside. No one knew when or where he died, but his wife died there.

Another person may have encountered a ghost, after drinking a spirit or two himself. One night, a guest came down to the front desk, about 2:30 in the morning. He stood very close to Jody, who could tell the man had been drinking, and asked, "Ish thissss place haunted?"

Jody said, "Yes I believe it is."

The man nodded his head and said, "That'ssss what I thought. Someone's been watching me," and went back to his room, which was number **307**.

Jody loves Astoria so much, he intends to stick around, even as a ghost.

Recent Happenings at the Hotel Elliott

I spoke with Sue and Ken Wilson, the hotel Managers, and Julie, the Events Coordinator and all around boss. Although the Wilsons were new to the hotel, they grew up on the Washington Coast. The Wilson's had not experienced anything strange, though they heard some guest and employee stories.

One night, a woman staying alone in **Room 405** called the front desk. She reported that there was an elderly gentleman, moving around in her room. She heard a voice from outside her room, calling for someone to come out. The man turned and walked out, through the door. The night auditor could not think of anything more to do than make sure the guest had calmed down, and report the incident.

One of the housekeepers heard someone talking in a room, which her cleaning schedule said was vacant. The housekeeper called down to the front desk, verifying the room status before letting herself on. When she went in, the room was empty.

In July 2006, I was in the lobby talking with the Elliott's staff, when a guest told this story to my friend Ross Allison. She was visiting her friend, who stayed in **Room 306**. While the guest took a shower, the first woman laid on the bed, fully dressed, watching television. She became aware of a hand, rubbing the outside of her leg, although there was no one in bed with her. It felt like a man's hand. She did not feel that it was sexual, but more like a tentative test, to make sure she was really there. After a few minutes the sensation stopped. I learned that one of the housekeepers cleaned that room once, and went back inside to double check things. She found an imprint on the bed cover, as if someone had just sat down on it.

Julie came to Astoria after a couple of hurricanes

finally drove her out of the Caribbean. Julie's mother in law told her that the Elliott Hotel was haunted, before Julie got the job. During her interview, Julie asked if the Elliott was haunted, and the manager admitted that there were some odd things about the hotel. Julie once lived in a house that was REALLY haunted (whater that means.) So to her, the things that have gone on at the Elliott Hotel are pretty mild and not at all frightening.

The most memorable event Julie had to share was on the 3rd floor outside **Room 307**, near the maid's closet. When she looked down the hallway, she saw the shadows of children against the wall, as if they were running down the hallway, around the corner. She thought it was a trick of light that she did not see the children themselves. It did not occur to her that there was nowhere for the children to run into to hide. She just thought these children were guests. A week or two later, a guest staying on the third floor complained to her that they heard children playing in the hallway. Whenever the guest opened the door to shush the children, they found the hallway empty.

Another thing I noticed when I visited the Hotel Elliott had to do with the room keys. Like most modern hotels, all of the rooms use magnetic cards to lock and open. All of the 07 and 08 numbered rooms (207, 208, 307, 308, etc.) seem prey to electromagnetic disturbances. The front desk staff frequently find themselves having to charge fresh cards for rooms which opened with the old one a few minutes earlier. This could be a normal problem with wiring. Right?

Brenda worked in laundry and housekeeping. She has seen what she thinks were people walking by, but when she concentrated on them, she realized that they were really spirits. She usually saw something white and misty in the laundry room, in the basement. She thought this could have been one of the Elliott ladies. One day, Anna was on housekeeping and she saw a figure in the cigar bar glass. She was not the only one

The Wine Bar

The Wine Bar is in the hotel basement. The best way to get there is by the elevator. The cigar bar was created when the staff set up several glass panels and a ventilation system to remove the cigar smoke without disturbing bar patrons. One evening Julie got off the elevator, turned around and saw something reflected in the cigar bar window. And then, it disappeared. It could have been a human figure, or something else. Julie's description is similar to Anna's sighting. She admits that at night the wine bar is a bit strange, and it could have been a trick of the light... Another employee took pictures in the basement, some of which contained many orbs.

I look forward to hearing more about the Hotel Elliott; perhaps it even has a curse? Chester Trabucco told me that after the tragic death of Mr. Elliott, the last two owners died within six months of selling the hotel. Chester vowed that he will sell the hotel when he reaches the age of 90.

The Heritage Museum 1618 Exchange Street

This museum was built in 1904, as Astoria's City Hall. Like most public buildings of that period, there are very high ceilings, and open spaces. The Neo-Classical building served many purposes. It was a temporary jail with holding cells, the library, a USO Club, and the Columbia River Maritime Museum. After the construction of the new Maritime Museum, the Clatsop County Historical Society turned it into the Clatsop County Heritage Museum.

I have heard rumors of some kind of haunting there, but only one witness told me of her experience. Early in 2000, Joan was a volunteer there. She walked by some of the jail cells on the first floor. She heard someone talking, and turned around, calling for her husband. There was no answer.

She found her husband, and asked him what he wanted. He replied that he had not called her. She did not leave though she felt like it. She always had what she called a creepy feeling when she walked by the old jail cells. That was the only thing that really bothered her.

Cemetery Ghosts

Some ghost hunters have visited the Pioneer Cemetery near Camp Rilea and captured what they believe were ghost orbs of light in photographs.

The Clatsop County Historical Society had an annual Halloween event called the Talking Tombstones in the old city cemetery. Volunteers and historians stood by the tombstones of past residents, reciting stories about some of the better known, and some lesser known townspeople. In their second year, 2005, there were 600 visitors to the event, which some have called edu-tainment

Underground (Shanghai Tunnels) Astoria

There were no "Shanghai Tunnels" in 19th Century Astoria. Most of 19th Century Astoria was built on piers, the fishing boat and cannery wharves, as well as warehouses, ship chandlers, bars and boarding houses. All the land north of Commercial Street was under water at high tide, and the buildings there stood on pilings, with open spaces underneath. Crooked tavern owners usually kept a rowboat tied up underneath the pier. When they wanted to Shanghai sailors, they lured the men in a backroom of the tavern. When he stood on a trapdoor concealed there, the Tavernier tripped a latch, and the sailor fell into the boat. If the fall did not disable the sailor, a bullyboy in the boat would.

After the fire of 1922, most of the city was in ruins. Just like the buildings, the fire destroyed most of Astoria's roads. Commercial Street was built on pilings driven into the soil, covered with boards, which were then paved with blacktop. The fire spread under the road, along the pilings. It became so hot that the blacktop caught fire. When Astoria rebuilt itself, the people dumped fill in the old roadbeds, and in the open spaces north of Commercial Street. Like Old Seattle, the ground floor sidewalks were built over the empty space created by the new raised roadbeds.

This created a series of tunnels, which connected the basements of the new buildings, running parallel to the streets. Visitors today can identify these tunnels by the purple glass on the sidewalk, which provided light to the basements. This happened late in Astoria's history, after the time when ship's captains needed to Shanghai sailors. So people have told me. Over the years, most of the businesses with basements connected to the tunnel system have blocked up their entrances, to keep out vagrants and thieves.

Rosebriar Inn Bed & Breakfast

The Rosebriar is the former residence of a prominent Astoria banker, Mr. Patton. Unlike many of the haunts I have found, there does not seem to be anything evil or mysterious about his life. Well, no more evil or mysterious than any banker who lived through the Great Depression. Mr. Patton built this mansion in 1902, and lived there until he died in 1952. His son sold it to an order of Catholic Nuns, who turned the mansion into their nunnery. This order moved in 1972, selling the building and other holdings. The building sat vacant for some time, before becoming Astoria's first Bed and Breakfast hotel in the 1980s

During a recent remodel, the owners kept the original wood paneling in the main room, as well as the front desk, and a decorative creek and shrine added by the nuns. The Pattons built a small ballroom in the house, which the nuns turned it into a chapel. It had stained glass windows, which the nuns kept, but changed by adding glass crosses in the middle of the original design. The current owners kept the confessional booth, and converted the attic into a master suite. The carriage house, which predated the mansion was also turned into a suite.

In 2006, my friend Laurie from the Officer's Inn became manager, and welcomed me for a night. Too bad my meager publishing budget could not afford the Carriage house, which had an indoor hot tub. I stayed in one of the normal guest rooms, which was furnished nicer than it had been when a lonely nun lived there. There were rumors of ghosts, perhaps some residue of the nuns, or the rich banker, refusing to leave his fine home. The earlier innkeepers discouraged any talk or publicity of paranormal events. Laurie and I took a tour, and discussed the house and perhaps a few ghosts.

After the tour, I talked with Laurie, and her housekeeper, Janice. They both had stories to share, even though Laurie started in July 2006, and Janice in June. Neither one had shared their experiences with each other before. Laurie went first.

She visited the Rosebriar before taking the job, and always had a peaceful feeling when she visited. After moving in, she had an experience in the kitchen. It was around 9:30 in the evening.

She thought it could have been shadows, but... She

was making coffee, and put the grounds into the maker, when out of the corner of her eye she thought she saw a nun. The woman was standing by the garbage can, then turned and disappeared. Laurie could not see the woman's face because her habit overshadowed her features. Strangely, the full habit was light blue in color. Laurie had never seen a blue habit.

In a separate incident, a couple stayed in Room 9. The next morning the woman came downstairs, and asked Laurie if she knew that they had "a visiting nun at the house."

Laurie repeated it as a question, "A visiting nun?"

The guest replied, "Yes, a visiting nun, I've actually seen her walking down the hallway."

Laurie replied, "we had a reunion of nuns here, is that what you are referring to?"

"No," the woman said, "This was an image I saw." She was very definite it was a ghostly nun. Laurie asked if she could describe any colors, hoping the woman also saw a blue habit. The woman described a normal black and white habit. The guest did not say whether this was on the second or first floor. She had known that the building had been a

nunnery before. Did this create some kind of subconscious illusion in the woman's mind? Perhaps, but what could have triggered it?

I found out later from paranormal researcher Jeff Belanger that it is not unusual to see a blue habit in a nunnery. Depending on the level of training and commitment of the woman; a Postulate nun in training wears a blue habit, a novice wears a white habit, and so on. So this ghostly woman was just entering holy orders. I wonder if she continued on?

Before I interviewed Laurie and Janice, they took me on a tour of the top floor of the Rosebriar. The owners turned the Rosebriar's attic into a suite with a magnificent view of the Astoria Harbor. While we were admiring the view, we all heard the front door slam shut. Janice hurried downstairs to greet any guests. She returned a few minutes later, and told Laurie, "It happened again."

I looked at Laurie for an explanation. She told me that when the two of them were away from the front desk, they would hear the front door slam shut. They could sometimes feel the vibrations. In many cases, there was no one there. Was this a prank?

Janice was irritated by the ghosts. In addition to the door slamming, she had trouble keeping bars of soap in some of the rooms. As housekeeper, she made sure that each room was done up just so. (As we toured the building, Janice and Laurie talked about whether the pillows on the beds were face up or down. As a man, they all looked the same to me...) I believe Janice when she talked of cleaning a room and laying out fresh linen and soap, only to return a few minutes later, finding the soap had vanished. Room 4 seemed to be a center for the infamous missing soap mystery. Janice also felt someone was watching her when she was alone in the hotel.

Laurie was a little surprised at this, and asked Janice why she did not mention it sooner. Janice told her that she kept quiet, because she did not want to frighten Laurie with any stories. The two of them only shared experiences when I was there. Laurie thought that the ghost liked Janice, and was constantly playing tricks on her.

I received an email from a woman named Joyce, who had lived at the Rosebriar, when it was the Phoenix House, a girls home. She wrote to me that she had visited recently, and heard about my book. As a girl, one of Joyce's duties was to clean up the foyer. One morning, she looked up from her work and saw what she first thought was smoke in the living room. It condensed or turned into the figure of a man, sitting in a chair. He seemed solid, and she remembered his old-fashioned business suit. He was smoking a pipe, and she noticed the shiny pocket watch hanging from his vest. As quickly as he appeared the man vanished.

Prior to receiving this email, my friend Karan visited the Rosebriar with me, and mentioned feeling a presence in the living room.

The living room at the Rosebriar Inn

After my visit, AGHOST, visited the Rosebriar and detected several layers of spirits, possibly from each set of occupants. They went in to their investigations cold, I did not share my interview results with them. It did not take Stephanie and Jody long to find a presence in the kitchen. They both felt it was that of a woman, along with a sensation of peace. Was this the nun Laurie had encountered? They felt the nun was named Josephine or Josephina. So far, they have not been able to contact the order to see if a past Reverend Mother had had that name.

The kitchen stairs were a different matter. Instead of a peaceful presence, Jody felt that some kind of tragedy happened there. Did someone fall down the stairs, or were they pushed. Fortunately, there was no spirit trapped there, just the residual energy of the fall.

As they walked around the house, perhaps the most energetic place was Room 4. Jody went to the window and channeled some kind of anxiety from a girl, who was afraid that "he" was coming home. Was it the banker's daughter, a nun, or from the time it was a girl's school? Jody felt there was some kind of verbal abuse, but also a strange connection with Room 5. As she went from Room 4 to 5, she heard a tapping noise, like Morse code. Could the occupants of the two rooms have communicated with each other by tapping out messages?

Altar outside the Rosebriar

They detected a male presence around the house,

perhaps a house worker, gardener, who was still intent on looking after things. There was a bench in the entry room to the Rosebriar, which had been in the chapel. When she sat on it, Jody could hear the sound of women's voices singing. Had she tapped into the nun's singing at their prayers? She told me she could have listened to it for hours. Jody paused near a closet, that exuded happiness. She could almost hear the sound of girls laughing as they came in from the outside, hanging up their clothing, gossiping.

The Tiny Victorian Lady

In addition to working at the Hotel Elliot, Jody talked about his historic home, along Alameda Avenue. It was a fine Victorian, built for one of Astoria's early families. It was on the National Register of Historic Places. Jody did not think the place was haunted until he took a picture of it with his digital camera. At first he did not notice anything odd, until he started zooming in on the windows. He saw a tiny woman in a Victorian dress and hat standing at the front window, looking outward. It could have been a real person, except she was transparent.

The previous owners did not say anything about it being haunted. When Jody and his wife toured the house, they found an old poster in the basement, a picture of a rose. He took that as a sign that the transparent woman wanted them to buy the house.

An odd thing happened when they moved in. They found candle wax dripped all the way up the stairs, and a candle sitting on the window at the top of the stairs, melted. A strange greeting. If their ghost was upset, she found ways to let Jody know that too.

Jody and his wife lived a quiet life, and they did not fight with each other very often. In the two years they lived there, the house witnessed four arguments. When they fought, it apparently upset their Victorian Lady. Shortly after the arguments, Jody heard a popping sound, and when he

investigated, he found the candles, which had been in holders on the piano, sitting several feet away. He lived there for some time, restoring what he could, but eventually sold it. Although he got a good price for the house, I think he misses his view of the harbor very much.

The Lion?

When Ana was 15 years old, she stayed at a friend's house. It was an old Victorian house on 26th Street. She stayed up late, reading a book, and heard what sounded like a lion or monster's roar. She got up and ran out of the house.

Chapter 5
Warrenton and Hammond

Fort Stevens State Park, Warrenton, Oregon

The primary tourist attractions at Fort Stevens State Park are the empty concrete bunkers that once housed the two big guns at Battery Russell. Tourists are unaware of the fact that there are several other gun emplacements nearby that are not part of the state park, or that the original gun emplacements at Fort Stevens date to the Civil War. Or that the gun emplacements are haunted.

During the War of 1812 British warships blockaded the mouth of the Columbia River. This was a lesson United States politicians and military planners did not forget. In 1840, they discussed plans to establish United States Army forts at the mouth of the Columbia River, but nothing was done until the 1860s. The Civil War motivated the War Department to look to the security of the Union in the Pacific. Confederate cruisers had attacked Union shipping in the Pacific. They may have been sheltering at the British naval base in nearby Victoria, Canada. With these potential threats, the Army ordered the construction of two forts to guard the mouth of the Columbia River.

In the summer of 1863 Captain George Elliot began work that took nearly two years to finish. He constructed roads, earthworks, and emplacements for over 40 guns at Fort Stevens. Only 29 cannons were mounted in January of 1865. The guns, some of which were cast in the War of 1812, remained in place until the turn of the century, when the War Department ordered the construction of new guns.

In 1995, when Robyn was 15, she and her family camped at Fort Stevens. They had been there many times, but had not heard of any ghost stories before this vacation. One day they took a walk along the fortifications, and approached the Civil War earthworks.

Out of the corner of her eye Robyn saw a figure. She turned and saw a man wearing what she believes to have been a Civil War uniform. She distinctly remembered seeing a pillbox cap. They made eye contact, he saluted her, and then disappeared. He was in color, looked normal, solid, or nearly so. Her family was walking behind her. When they caught up, she asked her father if he had seen someone on the earthworks ahead of her. He said he did not see anyone. When she told him what happened, he told her she was crazy.

In spite of thinking her crazy, Robyn's father took her to the visitors center and told them about the incident, asking if the area was haunted. The people there acted surprised, saying no one had ever mentioned ghosts there before.

The Watchman

There were several batteries with gun emplacements constructed at Fort Stevens, they included Lewis, Walker, Pratt, Freeman, Smur, Clark and Russell. The last bunker and gun emplacements to be finished were Battery Russell. The two 10 inch guns of the battery were finished and in place by 1908. The guns were designed to fire a 617 pound shell 16,290 yards or roughly 9 miles! The batteries of Fort Stevens watched the Pacific Ocean for 40 years before they were called to duty.

On the 21st of June 1942, a Japanese submarine commanded by Captain Meji Tagami surfaced off the coast and fired several rounds at Fort Stevens from her deck gun. The closest shell hit the beach 300 yards in front of Battery Russell. This was the first instance of United States soil being attacked by a foreign enemy in the 20th Century.

In 1947, the gun emplacements were decommissioned and the guns removed. A few years later Fort Stevens State Park was established. Most of the visitors at Fort Stevens are there during daylight hours, but some visitors stay to watch the sun set over the horizon. A few of them have been treated to other sights and sounds. People walking along the old road near Battery Russell have heard the sound of a metallic ringing or clanging, like a swinging chain or metal banging on metal.

The sight of a flashlight usually accompanies this sound, as if it is lighting a path along the road. The light and

sound will approach people on the road and get so close that the tourists have seen the outline of a man, holding the flashlight. At that point, the light and noise always cease. Some people think that this may be the ghost of a park night watchman or guard patrolling the road.

The Officer's Inn Bed & Breakfast

As its name suggests, the Officer's Inn was built between 1904 and 1905 as housing for military officers serving at Fort Stevens. It was one of the first residences built. Other buildings, such as a hospital, and stockade, or jail, soon followed. After WWII, the Army sold the building to the school district, which used it as a rental property. The school district sold it, and it changed hands several times. In 2001 or 2002, the Oregon State Parks bought the building, and used it as a rental home and B&B. In 2005, the state sold the house to Steve Nerding, who continued to operate it as a B&B.

Like most military houses, except for general officers quarters, it was a duplex, with each half the mirror image of the other side. The Officer's Inn is quite a large building, and senior officers, such as Colonels and their families lived there. Each half of the duplex included space for servant's quarters and a back staircase, although not all of the officer's were rich enough to hire servants. There were rich families whose children joined the Army and served, by tradition. If they lived well, it was because they had some secondary income. If they did not have another source of wealth, they had to put on a front.

The Officer's Inn former innkeeper Laurie told me that a woman who had lived there as a child visited once. The woman said they were so poor they hung sheets up over the windows instead of curtains. I also interviewed Laurie about strange things that happened at the Officer's Inn, a day or two ahead of my friends of AGHOST. Although Laurie did not think she was psychic, she seemed to have enough experiences to qualify as one.

When Laurie started working at the Officer's Inn, whenever she walked by the pantry, she smelled formaldehyde. She kept on asking people if they were bothered by the smell. No one seemed to notice it. After a few weeks, the smell went away. Laurie found out later, that when the house was originally built, it was occupied by one or two doctors. Laurie wondered if the formaldehyde was associated with the time that doctors had lived there. I wonder whether medical supplies were stored in there.

The week Laurie arrived, she was nervous about staying there alone, when no guests were there. She went to bed around 10 in the evening. Her rooms were in the servant's quarters on the north side of the building. She had her own separate entrance with a porch, close to the car park. After Laurie turned off the television, everything was very quiet. In the sudden silence, she heard the sound of a key being put into the lock on her outside door. The sound was slow and deliberate, if that metaphor is possible. To Laurie, it sounded as if someone pushed the key in slowly, so that she heard the sound of each tooth on the key as it slipped between the tumblers of the lock.

Laurie got up and looked out her window. She could see her private entrance. There was no one there. It only took a few seconds between the key being inserted into the lock, and her looking outside. This was not time enough for someone to walk away or hide. Laurie stayed awake for several minutes; her light on, cell phone in hand, waiting for a burglar to try to get into the house. She hoped it was someone playing a prank on her.

After a half hour, nothing happened. She went back to bed and somehow made it back to sleep. The next morning, she thought about what had happened. She remembered the sound of the key going into the lock, and how odd it sounded. The only conclusion she could reach was that someone had a skeleton key and deliberately tried to scare her. After several months at the Officer's Inn, she reached an opposite paranormal conclusion. Rather than trying to get into the building, whatever entity was there was trying to make Laurie welcome, by locking the door, making sure she was safe for the night.

She took me on a tour of the house, and its many rooms. She described an interesting haunting. To let guests enjoy the decor of the B&B, she left the doors to unoccupied rooms open. Several times guests told her that as they walked by one or two of the empty rooms, they saw people, or the outlines of people out of the corner of their eyes. When the guests investigated, they found the room empty. The General's Room was particularly active. As we continued our walk, Laurie pointed out a bedspread that was rumpled, as if someone had sat on it.

I did not think this was unusual, and said so. She told me that she had just cleaned the room, and always made sure that the bedspreads were smooth and tight on top of the bed. As we wandered around, we found several bedspreads in the same condition. Was she mistaken, or were the spirits aware of our impending investigation? Ross Allison and several investigators from AGHOST arrived the next day. We spent most of the day in Astoria, visiting several haunts and just enjoying walking around the city. We returned to the Officer's Inn later in the evening.

Laurie's second experience was in the basement with her friend, Suzanne. They were in the basement, talking about the noises old buildings had, paranormal and just creaking. Suddenly they felt a presence, and heard loud

noises. These noises came from the old furnace, which even though it was not turned on, it began clicking and clanking on its own.

One day, Laurie's mother was sitting at the dining room table in the northern dining room. There were several people in the house, but Laurie's mother was alone at that time. Around 10 in the evening, she looked up and saw a man walking through Laurie's quarters. The man wore an old fashioned fishing cap, and he walked from the kitchen sink, across her quarters, toward her bedroom. The man moved in a way that suggested he was sneaking, or trying to avoid being seen. Her mother yelled, and Laurie joined her. By then the man had vanished, and Laurie never saw him.

Murder Mystery Night

In June 2006, Laurie put on a Murder Mystery Night at the Officer's Inn. This is a parlor game, where people arrive at a party dressed in period clothing, and act out parts in a murder mystery. Of course, one of the guests is "murdered," and another is the murderer. It is up to the rest of the guests to play their parts, and find out who the murderer is. Laurie was happy with the way the game began. There were nearly 30 guests. The game called for a séance, where a Ouija board would spell out the name of the murderer. Like many people, Laurie had played around with a Ouija board when she was a teenager, and vowed never to use one again.

The game called for Laurie, as the host to use the Ouija board. She held onto the pointer, and started spelling out the name of the killer: L A R R Y. She moved the pointer around, with the help of another guest. Things started right, she got out an L, followed by an A, but when she moved the pointer to the letter R, it moved against her pressure to stop on the letter U. The message now read, L A U, not L A R. Laurie looked at the guest; only she could have forced the pointer to the wrong letter.

"Did you moved it to a "U?" Laurie asked.

The guest was surprised, and said no. The guest was not in on the "spirit message," and did not know what letter was next. Laurie kept going, using greater force to spell out LARRY. They talked later, and both noted they felt a kind of coldness on their fingertips, which touched the pointer.

An interesting twist to this murder mystery was that Laurie was indeed the murderer. According to the script, Laurie had originally been a man, who had a sex change operation, and changed names from Larry to Laurie. Did the ghost figure it out before the guests?

The AGHOST Investigation

The day after I interviewed Laurie, a team from AGHOST arrived. The team included a psychic, who went through the building with Laurie. After a while, Laurie separated from the group, and came down into the parlor where I was sitting with my wife Janine and friend Paul. Laurie was upset. I think that she and the AGHOST sensitive shared some psychic vibes, which had never happened to Laurie before. Laurie told us she was afraid, she could feel the house waking up to all the activity, and Laurie did not know what would happen. Because I am not psychic, there is normally no way that I can verify this kind of thing or not

That night was different. Laurie stood at the parlor entrance, never coming into the room. After talking to us a couple of minutes, she went to the kitchen to make some tea. A few seconds after she left, I noticed that the room became several degrees colder. There was no breeze, yet I felt a wave of coldness. I was sitting furthest away from the entrance, and I felt the cold start at my foot, and move up my leg, until my entire body was in the area of coldness. I looked at Janine and our friend Paul.

It was just like a horror movie. We all looked at each other in silence for several seconds. In these circumstances, who wants to admit something like this strange happening, even if you are there ghost hunting?

Janine spoke first, saying she noticed the temperature drop. I think she was relieved that Paul and I agreed with her. We sat for a few minutes, discussing what kind of mundane things might have caused this. The front door was open, and it was after dark and cool outside. However, I did not notice any draft. A draft would not have progressed slowly into the room. After a few minutes, the temperature warmed up. The next morning we got together over breakfast and shared observations from the entire team

Over breakfast, we listened to the observations of the psychic, Merlyn. She had an unusual practice of drawing sketches of what she saw or felt. She told us that as soon as she arrived, she noticed a little girl looking at her from a second floor window. The girl had long hair, done up in curls. They investigated, and found it was a linen closet.

This was the linen room window on the second floor, south side. Oddly, this is the only window where the window frame has never been painted. I noticed this window on my tour with Laurie, and there is something a little bit different in its design than the other windows. Had this been a nursery some time in the past?

Merlyn sensed another ghost, a woman associated with the little girl. She also felt the presence of a man in the house. She showed us a picture of a high dress boot, emphasizing how shiny it was. The boot design she drew had a leather flap that went over the shin, rather than lacing up the front, like most modern boots. It was reminiscent of the old doughboy or Mounties boots you sometimes see in movies. She also described a long wool jacket and cotton pants. It was vague, a cloak type jacket. I could not identify it with any particular uniform used between WWI and WWII.

From the Commander's room, Merlyn looked out the window and saw soldiers in khaki uniforms, standing in formation. Did she know that the open playground in front of the Officer's Inn had been a parade ground a hundred years earlier? In the Sergeant's room, she felt some kind of energy building up, and noted that there was some energy on one of the staircases.

This was the same place Laurie told me about the night before, where she had her psychic shock. Merlyn said she felt dizzy, just as Laurie did. Merlyn heard the sound of the rocking chair, rocking back and forth. She also heard the sound of footsteps walking across a wooden floor, even though the floor was carpeted. This coincided with an observation of Laurie's, the day before where the rocking chair and table in the room was moved from one part of the room to the other. Even though Laurie was the only one who was in the house.

Merlyn stayed in the General's Room that night, and described what she experienced. She heard a rattling from one end of the bed, across the room. The noise sounded like someone was going through her belongings. She got up and looked, nothing was moving although the sound was still there. She thought it might have been the radiator but it was not; it had been disconnected.

Merlyn fell asleep reading, and dreamed of the little girl. She not just one girl, but two identical twins. Merlyn felt that if they were twins, one of the girls had died in the house. The building owner said that he had some records, and knew the names of the officers, but not the children.

The discussion continued about the basement. Joey felt she had a name for the girl, **Clair** or **Clara**. Two AGHOST members claimed that they heard a female voice say, "Hello" to them in the basement. Joey tried to get any ghost voices on her tape recorder.

She asked: "why are you still here?"

"I got lost," the voice responded.

Joey asked, "Where is your mom?"

"She left me." A few minutes later, there was a child's sigh or whimper.

Joey noted that the recorder acted strange from room to room. When they were upstairs it seemed to record things normally, or even on the loud side. When they were in the basement, the recordings were low toned, and muffled.

While in the basement, Ross Allison asked a question, "If you want to communicate with us, tap twice."

They heard a single tap. Ross asked, "one more time please."

But there was only silence. Then one of the team member's headlamp went out. It became cold. The person holding the microphone felt the hair on her hand go up, from the chill or fear. They saw a shadowy figure standing by the basement doorway. It was not perfectly solid, it undulated like a mist. It dissipated after a few seconds. With that, the investigation ended, as if it used up its stores of energy..

Chapter 6

Other Haunts Nearby

Louie at the Lamplighter Inn (Seaview, Washington)

The Lamplighter Inn has been a part of the Long Beach community for over 125 years. This has been time enough to accumulate a number of ghosts. There are certainly some strange goings-on there. The primary candidate for some of the more physical phenomenon is the late Louie Sloan. Sloan owned the restaurant/lounge for decades before he sold it in 1963. After that he was a regular fixture in the bar until he died in 1977 at the age of 80. Strange poltergeist activity began shortly after that.

Shortly after Louie's death Jenita VanBuskirk was closing the lounge for the night. Two people playing pool delayed her. They ignored her repeated statements that the bar was closing, so she turned off the lights over the pool table. She walked away from the light switch and was surprised when the lights came back on. She walked back to the switch and found it was still in the off position.

In 1990, Mary Smith was working at the lounge. There was only one patron in the bar that night, sitting at the bar. Smith heard a clicking noise and looked at the pool table. She watched as the balls began moving across the table, bumping into each other. Their collision had made the noise she heard. This continued for several minutes. Lamplighter employees and patrons accumulated many stories about strange happenings.

They felt that it was no coincidence that all of this began shortly after Louie's death. Much of the phenomena ceased or at least slowed down after Louie returned to the Lamplighter; at least part of him did. When he died, Louie was cremated at Penttila's Chapel by the Sea funeral home. No one collected his ashes, which were placed in the attic along with those of 50 other people. In 1992, the owners of the Lamplighter accepted the urn containing Louie's ashes and placed it in the lounge. I received word in 2005, that Louie still makes himself known from time to time. Everyone believes that the permanent move pleased Louie and he has come home to rest.

The Knappton Pest House Museum, (Knappton, Washington)

The little town of Knappton, Washington is located on the north bank of the Columbia River, opposite Astoria. What is interesting historically, and perhaps paranormally is that Knappton was the Ellis Island of the Columbia River; the United States Immigration Pest House.

In the later 19th Century, international shipping brought many exotic goods and people to the United States. Along with the people and their goods came unwanted immigrants, like rats, and the germs they carried. Most of the people coming into the Pacific Northwest were English, Japanese, German, Scandinavian, Peruvians, etc. After 1880, few Chinese were allowed into the United States, because of the 1880 Chinese Exclusion Act. Sometimes the people themselves were disease carriers.

One of the most feared diseases was the bubonic plague, which had a mortality rate of nearly 70 percent. A close second was smallpox, followed by other less fatal, but still feared diseases, like yellow fever, typhus, and cholera. With all of the ports along the West Coast, the United States government contended with various outbreaks before regulating immigration and health inspections.

In 1891, Congress mandated health inspections at centralized locations. If a ship was not inspected there first, it would not be allowed to dock anywhere in the United States. The United States Public Health Services Commission Corps performed these health inspections, under the Surgeon General. Ellis Island opened in 1892. Another inspection facility at Port Townsend opened around that time, as did one in San Francisco. The merchants along the Columbia River complained that they had to wait extra time for ships to be inspected at these ports before sailing up the Columbia, so the facility in Knappton was built in 1899.

The ship owners had to pay for their ships to be inspected. They did not care so much about the well being of their passengers or their crew as much as their profits. If the public health service found too many pests, the quarantine could last several days or weeks, which cost the ship owners money. If the ship was clean, the inspection, quarantine, and fumigation process would be limited to 48 hours.

To avoid this loss of money, ship's captains sometimes cast sick sailors and passengers adrift, or simply dumped them overboard as the ship approached port. The Public Health Service enforced a policy in the 1920s raising health and food standards onboard ships, pointing out that healthy passengers and crew cut down on the time in quarantine, which made for a bigger profit.

Even though ships eventually unloaded in Astoria or Portland, they docked first in Knappton for the health inspection. This policy stopped any diseased person from jumping ship in Astoria and hiding before the inspection. Of course, the people in Knappton were not pleased with this, but the Astorians had more political power at that time. The facility the government chose had been a cannery, which was perfectly suited to the sanitation and fumigation process.

While the facility operated, ships docked at a pier some distance from the shore, and everyone offloaded. They did not leave the pier, but walked to a building constructed along the wharf. The inspection building had separate men and women's sections, and probably had male and female inspectors. People stripped, showered, and doctors inspected them as their clothing and luggage was taken away. People went from station to station, getting *cleaner* as they went along. Once they passed inspection, the passengers collected their sanitized luggage and left the pier, while the ship was fumigated. They waited the two day clearance period on a decommissioned battleship anchored at the pier. Many enjoyed a higher standard of hygiene and food than they had in their country of origin.

The fumigation process was very simple, yet effective. All the openings and portals were sealed, and the Health Service supervised workers burning big vats of sulfur on the ship. The hydrogen sulfide killed the vermin onboard. Later they used cyanide gas. Baggage and clothing was not fumigated. The huge pressure cooking machines in the abandoned cannery were converted into driers, with racks for stacking luggage inside. The hot dry air inside these driers killed any vermin or germs. After this process ended, passengers and sailors transferred back to their ship, which sailed to Astoria.

The Health Service detained any sick or possibly contagious people at the facility. Oddly, the Health Service sent very serious cases to the Columbia Hospital in Astoria on board the ship *Electro*. The doctors did not live in Knappton; but in Astoria, where they took better care of patients. Because of that, there were no records of patients dying at the Knappton Pest Facility. This Pest House facility was also called a *Lazaretto*, from the man Lazarus, who died of pestilence, and was brought back to life.

There were several buildings for the health workers, as well as the isolation hospital, designed to house 20 people. It was "H" shaped, with a main entrance in the middle of the building, opening into a large ward. There were two smaller isolation wards at either end. Each isolation ward had two rooms each. Although people could enter the isolation wards from the main room, each room had its own separate entrance. The only time it was filled was in the 1920s, when Knappton burned to the ground, and the townsfolk stayed in the hospital until they rebuilt their homes.

By 1950, the main port of entry for the Columbia River was Portland. The Knappton facility was sold to a man who turned it into a sport fisherman's club. In the 1960s, the state highway cut through the middle of the facility, dividing the housing from the pier. Every winter storms pounded the old dock and the owner could not afford to repair it. Most of the pier rotted away, leaving the dolphin (joined pilings) sticking out of the water. The owner's daughter, Nancy Bell Anderson, a retired school teacher, turned the isolation hospital into a museum, to preserve the history of the area.

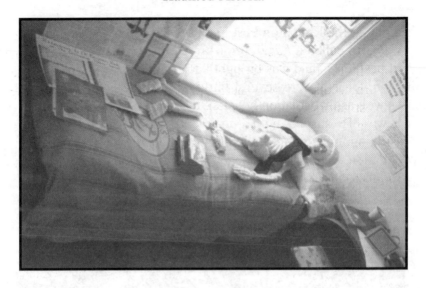

Does a patient still remain in the isolation ward?

A Haunted Hospital?

Neither Nancy nor her family had heard or seen anything strange in the old hospital. For several years, a retired epidemiologist from the Midwest rented one of the two isolation ward apartments for the summer. He sometimes dressed in period clothes, and volunteered to explain the facility to visitors. He never reported anything odd; however, one guest at the pest house some time before, had reported a feeling strange. He said that there was a presence observing him while he was there. It was not dangerous, just watchful.

Nancy and her family were amused and skeptical, but open enough to admit the possibility that something odd could be happening. In the late 1990s, a paranormal group approached Nancy, asking permission to investigate the facility. Her husband thought the idea was dumb, but he agreed to participate. The group arrived around twilight, set up some experiments and sensors, and left the building.

They put a cup of coffee in one of the isolation wards.

They marked a line on the cup of coffee to check its level and asked any entities to drink some. They also put a shot of bourbon on another table. Nancy told them that if the bourbon disappeared, her father was back. One of the investigators, a psychic saw a man with a mustache. They thought this was a caretaker at the property, based on a photo album Nancy showed them.

The group went down the beach, and one intuitive person, saw a woman dressed in 19th Century period clothing on the strand. This interested Nancy, as a teacher and historian.

In 1814, after the British took over the area, they sent several vessels to supply Fort George. The Chief Factor, Donald MacTavish, was preparing for the voyage when he and a friend went to a pub in Portsmouth. They met a serving woman, named Jane Barnes. The men persuaded the blue-eyed flaxen haired beauty to come along for the voyage... perhaps after a few drinks? She signed on as the ship's seamstress, on the *Isaac Todd*. Although the nearby town is known today as Knappton, the original land documents named it Todd's Bay.

The *Isaac Todd* anchored in the little bay with Donald MacTavish and his Jane. Part of Jane's compensation for coming along was a new wardrobe. MacTavish bought Jane, silks, plumes, and lace. Jane arrived at Fort George, where her presence caused a stir. MacTavish sent her to Todd's Bay, where she lived on the ship. She often walked the beach where the pest house was built, wearing her fine clothing. MacTavish visited her from time to time, until one stormy night, when his boat overturned, and he drowned. Perhaps Jane still walks the beach waiting for Mr. MacTavish.

Although some of the experiments sounded bizarre to Nancy, she complimented them on the serious way they conducted themselves. They were so intent on the readings from their scientific instruments that they did not examine the coffee cup they set out for the spirits. Nancy's daughter did, and said, "Mom, look at the coffee cup."

The level was down about three quarters of an inch. They examined the table around the cup. There was no evidence of a spill. The group left the owners a CD, with copies of their audio recordings. In one place, she laughingly admitted she may have heard the word, "coffee." She suggested that they were primed to hear that word because of the strange loss of the coffee in the cup.

Although quarantine and pest houses sound like the Middle Ages, it was less than a hundred years ago when the facility operated. Nancy showed me a yellow quarantine flag that she remembered a Liberian ship flew for several weeks, when it was quarantined in the Astoria harbor.

Bandage Man (near Cannon Beach, Oregon)

The bandage man is a creature that has passed from first hand accounts into a coastal legend with many different spins and variations in this story. It is unknown if he is a living being or a ghost. I have heard that Bandage Man is the ghost of an accident victim, perhaps a logger, who died while being driven into town. He may have been an escaped inmate from an insane asylum, living in the woods, who liked to eat dogs or sometimes just drink their blood. I have even heard that he may be a Sasquatch that somehow put on rags for clothing. I do not think that he has been described as a space alien. Yet!

Despite these mutations to the Bandage Man's origins, the story of his activities seems to be fairly straightforward. People driving into Cannon Beach from Highway 26 should be very careful when they reach the intersection of 26 with U.S. Highway 101. People driving that stretch of road at night in pick-up trucks or open top vehicles should beware. Bandage Man may jump in the back of their vehicle. He may pound on the cab of a truck, or break windows, scaring the drivers. Then he jumps out of the vehicle or simply disappears. He usually leaves behind a bloody bandage or the smell of rotting flesh.

I spoke with the Oregon State Police in Astoria. Their patrol area included Canon Beach. They have not had any calls about any strange hitchhikers near Cannon Beach for several years In his book, *Oregon's Ghosts & Monsters* Mike Helm includes a long tale about Bandage Man.

Tillamook Rock Lighthouse (Near Canon Beach, Oregon)

Between the isolation the Tillamook Rock enjoyed in prehistoric times and its present solitude, the Rock had an intense and important human occupation. Construction on the lighthouse was begun in 1879 and took nearly a year and a half to complete. It was dedicated in January of 1881 and operated until 1957. A small crew of light keepers led a lonely existence. Frequently a boat or ship with supplies and personnel would have to anchor just off shore of the island and have a derrick lift supplies off the deck and winch them up to the base of the lighthouse. The derrick was destroyed by a storm in 1934. The Lighthouse was shut off at midnight on 1 September, 1957 and sat vacant for decades.

The island where the Tillamook Rock Lighthouse stands has come full circle in spiritual terms. It was a sacred place to Native American's for hundreds, perhaps thousands of years. According to their legends, Elip Tillicum, powerful spirits, caused canoes to wreck on the rocky haunted island. This legend seemed to come true when construction began on the lighthouse. The Master Mason hired to oversee construction of the lighthouse was swept off the rock by a wave the day he landed to begin work. Today the island and lighthouse are again sacred; the lighthouse has been converted into a necropylon, a giant monument where cremated human remains are kept.

Mimi Morisette bought Tillamook Rock and the lighthouse in 1981. Work crews gutted the interior of the lighthouse, leaving only the spiral staircase leading to the top of the tower. They sealed and cemented all of the windows and other openings and installed shelving units to store cremated human remains. They still go out to the island when they can, to repair any storm damage to the structure as well as to ferry ashes to their final resting place.

Between the time when the lighthouse was vacated and its conversion there were a few visitors, mostly curiosity seekers like John Buckingham. In 1980, John contacted the owner of the Tillamook Rock, and received permission to visit the old lighthouse. He chartered a twenty three foot boat from Seaside and quickly reached the island.

The boat circled the island, as John faced the real peril of trying to jump out of the boat onto the rock without getting washed away by waves. After a few practice half-jumps, he leapt out of the boat and safely clambered on the Rock. While avoiding large piles of seagull droppings John walked quickly to the open lighthouse. He found the furniture left behind warped, the paint peeling off the walls and all exposed metal turning into rusty scraps.

After looking at the ground floor of the lighthouse, he walked up the spiral staircase to the lantern room at the top of the lighthouse. He reached the lantern room without hearing or seeing anything unusual. It was not until he reached the second floor landing that he heard the sound of a human voice, moaning in pain.

John was the only person on the island, there was nowhere for anyone to hide. He did not wait to investigate the sound; he hurried down the stairs and out of the lighthouse, slamming the door shut behind him. He signaled to the waiting boat and leapt aboard as soon as it came close to shore, perhaps the last person to hear the ghost.

INDEX

About the Author

Jefferson Davis was born in the Pacific Northwest, and has degrees in Anthropology and Archaeology. He has worked and traveled widely throughout Washington and Oregon. His background and curiosity about the paranormal heritage of the Northwest helped Jeff research and write six books on paranormal events of the region. He has contributed stories to the Weird US book, *Weird Hauntings*. He is currently writing *Weird Washington*.

He has appeared on the History Channel's series,

Haunted History and has been heard on *Coast-to-Coast AM* and the *Lou Gentile Show.* He worked as a creative consultant for the Lincoln County and Kutz Productions for the video, *Oregon Ghost Explorer.* Jeff has also been a guest on many of the Northwest's television and radio stations.

Jeff's website: *www.ghostsandcritters.com* is one of the oldest Internet website in the Pacific Northwest to give evidence of the paranormal in the region.

Jeff lives in Vancouver, Washington with his wife and two spoiled cats. His more mundane activities include teaching college part time and running his own small publishing business.

Other Books By Jeff Davis

Ghosts and Strange Critters of Washington and
Oregon

Ghosts, Critters and Sacred Places of
Washington and Oregon

Ghosts, Critters and Sacred Places of
Washington and Oregon II

Ghosts, Critters and Sacred Places of
Washington and Oregon III

A Haunted Tour Guide to the Pacific Northwest